OLIVER GOLDSMITH'S
THE CITIZEN OF THE WORLD

A STUDY

BY

HAMILTON JEWETT SMITH

ARCHON BOOKS
1970

824
G57 Cd

[*Yale Studies in English, Vol. 71*]

SBN: 208 00911 6
Library of Congress Catalog Card Number: 70-91190
Printed in the United States of America

TO MY MOTHER

PREFACE

Even those familiar with the erratic genius of Oliver Goldsmith cannot realize the extent of its vagaries until they have attempted to apply the methods of scholarly research to problems concerning him. A process of logical reasoning will hinder rather than guide the student who tries to follow the capriciousness of Goldsmith's mind, which will lead into the most sudden, unexpected channels. An equally perplexing obstacle placed in the way of verifying every fact is Goldsmith's unparalleled temperamental carelessness. There seems no end to the slips he made. Several times in the *Chinese Letters,* for example, he used the same number to designate different essays; and, in republishing the letters under the title, *The Citizen of the World,* he again made similar errors for still different papers. His most conspicuous mistake, found in the printing of the first draft of *The Traveller,* is due to a characteristic oversight. He failed to reverse the order of his pages before sending them to the printer. Thus the poem was published with the conclusion first, and proceeded with the most curious and illogical transition to the beginning, on the last page of the book. Such careless habits at first tax the patience of his reviewer sorely; they in time divert rather than worry him, and he comes to regard his search for facts in the spirit of a game, not unlike 'Hunting the Snark.' But, encouraged once or twice by a success which throws sudden light upon larger issues, he continues to pursue with pleasure the *ignis fatuus.*

Too little investigation has been made of Goldsmith's writings, and much remains to be done in interpreting his interesting genius. Since the late nineteenth century, when the studies of Peter Cunningham, Austin Dobson, and J. W. M. Gibbs appeared, there has been no new, important edition of *The Citizen of the World.* And each of these, even the excellent edition of Gibbs, left much work undone.

The correct dates and original order of appearance of all the essays are given accurately for the first time in the present study; hitherto scattered facts have been assembled, and much new material presented, which, I think, lends new significance to the *Chinese Letters.* I treat, especially, the circumstances which led to the printing of the essays, the history of their publication and that of the subsequent edition of *The Citizen of the World,* the Oriental influences and background, and the literary relations and sources. The investigation of the latter two points has been much more fruitful and significant than I had any reason to suspect at the outset of my study.

The original text in the *Public Ledger* has been used for this study, and collated with the texts of the first and third editions, which were the editions of the collected letters personally revised by Goldsmith. Gibbs alone, among the editors of *The Citizen of the World,* uses the newspaper version. His collation of the text does not aim to be thorough, and it makes many important omissions.

Editors have previously annotated Chinese and other Oriental allusions on the basis of books which appeared later than Goldsmith's letters. Such annotations, and the study of the Eastern background, are now made from books actually consulted by Dr. Goldsmith. And, in passing, numerous errors in dates and in other matters of fact have been corrected.

I do not hesitate to prophesy that scholars will from time to time find, in the most unexpected places, more sources of Goldsmith's writings, nor to add that the extent of his borrowings will increase the appreciation of his ability as a writer; for, to employ Johnson's words, he touched nothing that he did not adorn.

I desire to convey my thanks to Professor Chauncey Brewster Tinker, of Yale University, not only for suggesting the subject of this dissertation, and for his assistance and painstaking criticism, but even more for his encouragement as a teacher and friend. Under his guidance, scholarly research is an inspiration. I wish, also, to thank Dr. Joseph Brown, of Princeton, for reading my book, and for making valuable suggestions. My work has been greatly facilitated by the courtesy of Mr. Andrew Keogh, the Librarian of Yale University, and his staff, by the officials of the Harvard and Princeton University libraries, and by those of the British Museum. Especially I wish to record my gratitude to Professor Albert Stanburrough Cook, to whom Yale students owe so much.

How much I owe to my mother for the love of letters and of all things else that are good in life, I cannot express; for to her is due my growing appreciation of these things since my earliest childhood. To her devotion this effort and all future efforts of mine must always chiefly be due.

H. J. S.

Berkeley, California.

What am I?. . . . A man whose character may one of these days be mentioned with profound respect in a German comment or a Dutch dictionary; whose name you will probably hear ushered in by a Doctissimus Doctissimorum, or heel-pieced with a long Latin termination. . . . There will come a day, no doubt it will—I beg you may live a couple of hundred years longer only to see the day—when the Scaligers and Daciers will vindicate my character, give learned editions of my labours, and bless the times with copious comments on the text. You shall see how they will fish up the heavy scoundrels who disregard me now, or will then offer to cavil at my productions. How will they bewail the times that suffered so much genius to lie neglected. If ever my works find their way to Tartary or China, I know the consequence. Suppose one of your Chinese Owanowitzers instructing one of your Tartarian Chinnobacchi—you see I use Chinese names to show my own erudition, as I shall soon make our Chinese talk like an Englishman to show his. This may be the subject of the lecture:

> Oliver Goldsmith flourished in the eighteenth and nineteenth centuries. He lived to be a hundred and three years old, [and in that] age may justly be styled the sun of [literature] and the Confucius of Europe. [Many of his earlier writings, to the regret of the] learned world, were anonymous, and have probably been lost because united with those of others. The first avowed piece the world has of his is entitled an 'Essay on the Present State of Taste and Literature in Europe,'—a work well worth its weight in diamonds. In this he profoundly explains what learning is, and what learning is not. In this he proves that blockheads are not men of wit. and yet that men of wit are actually blockheads.

But as I choose neither to tire my Chinese Philosopher, nor you, nor myself, I must discontinue the oration in order to give you a good pause for admiration. . . .

I am ever wholly thine.

OLIVER GOLDSMITH.

CONTENTS

THE CITIZEN OF THE WORLD

CHAPTER I

The Growth of an Idea

Not unlike the sudden interest in those small islands of the South Seas which many books of travel bring to the modern reader, was the enthusiasm for the Orient that a similar flood of literature gave to the mid-eighteenth century Englishman. Just as we are receiving imaginative and colored accounts of the Marquesans, so he received descriptions of pretended realism concerning an Orient which existed largely if not wholly in fancy, with widely varying degrees of truth. It would be an unfortunate age that could not gain fresh tales of distant and strange peoples, about whom any fanciful account could be readily believed.

To the Londoner of 1860, if the true East was still unknown, a pseudo-Orient was no undiscovered land. Newspaper and magazines with Oriental tales, pseudo-Oriental letters, accounts of Eastern countries, innumerable works of history, travel, and fiction, brought him report of it. Few of the writers of the age neglected to tell him of it. The magical stories of the *Arabian Nights,* which had been first translated into English in the reign of Queen Anne, still held their fascination in the mid-century. Collins gave an exotic background to his early poetry in the *Persian Eclogues;* Hawkesworth wrote about the East in his *Adventurer,* giving to journalism the setting of the Orient; Lyttelton dealt with Eastern material in his epistolary essays, *Letters from a Persian in England to his friend in Ispahan.* From translations, as well, the subject received momentum; English versions were made of the French works by Marana, Gueullette, Montesquieu, and D'Argens which dealt with the Orient.[1] Dr. Johnson contributed numerous Oriental tales to the *Rambler* and the *Idler,* and in 1759 published *Rasselas,* the best known of the writings on Oriental subjects which flooded England.[2]

Of the Eastern countries, China was most described. It was visited by Jesuit missionaries and curious travelers. In every field of writing this country was discussed. The long histories by Du Halde and Le Comte were translated into English, and reprinted.[3] The journals of the day brought news of China to a wide range of people. Most numbers of the *Gentleman's Magazine,* the *British Magazine,* and the *Monthly Review* contained observations on this country. On the stage the subject was treated by Arthur Murphy in his

---

[1] Marana, Giovanni Paolo. *Letters writ by a Turkish Spy* . . . (trans. from the French) . . . 8 vols., London, 1687-1693. Twenty-second edition, 1734; . . . edition 1748; twenty-sixth edition, 1770. (For disputed authorship, see note, p. 39.)

Gueullette, Thomas Simon. *Chinese Tales* . . . London, 1725. *Mongul Tales* . . . London, 1736; second edition, 1743. *Tartarian Tales* . . . London, 1759. *Peruvian Tales* . . . fourth edition, London, 1764.

Montesquieu, C. de Secondat, Baron de. *Persian Letters Translated by Mr. Ozell.* London, 1730. Third edition, 1731; sixth edition, anon., Edinburgh, 1773.

Boyer (Jean Baptiste de), Marquis D'Argens. *Chinese Letters,* . . . now done in English . . . London, 1739.

[2] Johnson, Samuel. *The Rambler,* July 28, 1750; Oct. 30, 1750; May 11, 1751; Jan. 11, 1752; Feb. 29, 1752; March 3, 1752; also *The Idler,* Sept. 22, 1759; March 8, 1760; March 22, 1760.

The Prince of Abissinia [sic], *a Tale* [= Rasselas]. London, 1759. Second edition, 1759. Another edition, Dublin, 1759.

[3] See Boswell's *Life of Johnson,* ed. Hill, 1. 158; also note 2: 'Du Halde's description of China, was then publishing (A. D. 1738) by Mr. Cave in weekly numbers, whence Johnson was to select pieces for the embellishment of the *Magazine.* Nicholas. Boswell.' See also same, 2. 63, and index.

Orphan of China,[4] in fiction by Wilkinson in his translation of the Chinese novel, *Hau Kiou Chooan,* and by Percy in his edition of Chinese romances, which he collected under the title of *Miscellaneous Pieces relating to the Chinese;* in the field of scholarship, Sir William Jones, a friend of Dr. Johnson, published many volumes of investigation.[5] In his work on Oriental gardening, Chambers instructed the English public in the Chinese taste for decoration. But the interest in China perhaps reached its height when Horace Walpole, dictator of fashion, turned his attention temporarily to the Chinese. In letters to his friends he repeatedly reveals his interest in porcelain knickknacks and dragon-headed furniture, and comments seriously on art and decoration.[6] There are some fifty passages in which he discusses at greater or less length the beauties of things Chinese. In 1757, Walpole published a poetical tract, in which the critic, Xo-Ho, points out the errors of English ways by comparing them to Chinese ways.[7] This tract ran through five editions in a fortnight. So for a few years the maxims of Confucius were heralded by English writers as models of moral teaching; the precepts became bywords; and China itself was extolled as a remote, neglected land of strange fascination. During these years the most popular fad was the country of Confucius.

[4] *The Orphan of China* was first performed on April 21, 1759. Garrick and Mrs. Yates played the two principal characters, Zamti and Mandane.

[5] *Traité sur la Poésie Orientale; Dissertation sur la Littérature Orientale; Grammar of the Persian Language; Poeseos Asiaticæ Commentariorum Libri Sex; On the Chinese* (from *Asiatic Researches*) ; and many other works.

[6] *Letters,* ed. Mrs. Paget Toynbee, 2. 311, 334, 375, 433; 3. 4, 35, 97, 119, 130, 168, 179, 182, 248, 250, 302, 317, 328, 363; 4. 55, 72, 82, 394, 397, 414; 5. 149, 215, 247, 252, 384; 6. 39; 7. 277; 8. 418, 419; 9. 243; 10. 145, 391; 11. 58, 127, 248, 372; 12. 11.

[7] *A Letter from Xo-Ho, a Chinese Philosopher at London, to his friend Lien Chi at Pekin, 1757.*

This interest in China was not confined to literature; it extended into the social life of the people. Gardens in England were laid out in supposed Chinese fashion; ladies covered their mantels with idols, pagodas, and mandarins.[8] One writer said:[9]

> The simple and sublime have lost all influence almost everywhere, all is Chinese or Gothic; every chair in an apartment, the frames of glasses, and tables, must be Chinese; the walls covered with Chinese paper filled with figures which resemble nothing of God's creation, and which a prudent nation would prohibit for the sake of pregnant women.
>
> In one chamber, all the pagods and distorted animals of the east are piled up, and called the beautiful decorations of a chimney-piece; on the sides of the room, lions made of porcelain, grinning and misshapen, are placed on brackets of the Chinese taste, in arbors of flowers made in the same ware, and leaves of brass painted green lying like lovers in the shades of old Arcadia.
>
> Nay, so excessive is the love of Chinese architecture become, that at present the fox hunters would be sorry to break a leg in pursuing their sport in leaping any gate that was not made in the eastern taste of little bits of wood standing in all directions; the connoisseurs of the table delicacies can distinguish between the taste of an ox which eats his hay from a Chinese crib, a hog that is inclosed in a stye of that kind, or a fowl fattened in a coop the fabric of which is in that design, and find great difference in the flavor. . . .
>
> The Chinese taste is so very prevalent in this city at present, that even pantomime has obliged harlequin to seek shelter in an entertainment, where the scenes and characters are all in the taste of the nation.

[8] Cf. *The Citizen of the World* 3. *51-4.*

[9] John Shebbeare, *Letters on the English Nation: By Battista Angeloni, a Jesuit, Who resided many years in London. Translated from the Original Italian.* 1755. See Letter LVI.

Dozens of books on gardening, music, furniture, cookery, or architecture bore witness to the taste of the age for things Chinese.[10]

The condition of affairs in the England of 1760, with its renewed interest in the lands of the *Arabian Nights,* and its sudden craze for the novelties of China, made it particularly fitting that the young Goldsmith, desirous of attracting the attention of the London public, should, in the dignified guise of a mandarin philosopher, become the critic of his nation. A pseudo-letter serial printed in a London newspaper, having for its hero a Chinese who told strange tales of the East, who moralized, philosophized, and satirized, was to the English of this time a new kind of literature, which was then sure of popularity. Goldsmith would eagerly have seized upon such a plan if he had been able to realize its effectiveness at once; but formulating so fortunate a device was an evolution, and not a sudden inspiration. It was the combination of three elements which gave the great significance to the Chinese letters: their periodic appearance, pretended foreign nationality of the author, and Chinese subject-matter. The London public was satiated with periodic moral essays. Some novel scheme was needed to stimulate fresh interest. The pseudo-letter had long been popular in France, but, save in fiction and in the work of George Lyttelton, was not widely known

[10] See *World,* No. 12: 'Everything was Gothic, now it is Chinese'; also Nos. 26, 38, 59, 65, 117, 205;
Connoisseur No. 135:

> The trav'ler with amazement sees
> A temple, Gothic or Chinese;
> With many a bell and tawdry rag on,
> And crested with a wooden dragon.

Also see Nos. 65, 73; *Adventurer,* Nos. 109, 139; *Rambler,* No. 82; *Mirror,* No. 17; *Lounger,* No. 79. Also William Chambers, *Designs of Chinese Buildings,* etc., London, 1757; and Martha Conant, *The Oriental Tale in England,* pp. 223-5.

in England. To this novelty Goldsmith added the popular topic of China. Each of the elements was in itself old; each finds some parallel in other writings. The effective combination of the three components, which gave literary significance to Goldsmith's venture in journalism, was Goldsmith's own.

A series of events and suggestions from other writers, however, led up to the establishment of the Chinese-letter scheme in its final form. The author who had most to do with influencing Goldsmith in this direction was a man of wholly different character, whose influence on the eighteenth-century humorist has been little suspected, and never fully investigated. Voltaire pointed the way to the composition of his first prominent work.

Before showing concretely the extent of Voltaire's stimulus to the development of Goldsmith as an essayist, I wish to call attention to the more general influence which that distinguished French writer had upon the opinions of the almost unknown young Irishman. The one was a conservative, brought up in the orthodox opinions of a clergyman's household; the other a skeptic, with training in a different world. Yet, in his earliest days as a writer, Goldsmith drew widely on the learning of Voltaire. In composing *An History of England, in a Series of Letters from a Nobleman to his Son,* he transcribed freely from the pages of the *Histoire Universelle,* later known as the *Essai sur les Mœurs,* which had originally attracted much attention upon its appearance in 1753-4.[11] So it was not unfitting that in 1756, when a new Geneva edition of this work appeared, Goldsmith should review it at length, with high praise, in the *Monthly Review,*[12] August, 1757. He

---

[11] The discovery of Goldsmith's very extensive borrowings for his *History of England* was recently made by R. B. Crane and J. H. Warner. See *Modern Language Notes* 38. 65-76.

[12] See Goldsmith, *Works,* ed. Gibbs, 4. 277.

further showed admiration for Voltaire by reprinting numerous selections from his writings in the *Bee;* namely, on October 6, 1759, *A Letter from Voltaire to M. D'Arget, of Lausanne,* on October 13, 1759, *A Letter from Mr. Voltaire to Mr. Tiriot;* on October 20, 1759, *On Wit* (from the article *Esprit*) ; and, on November 10, 1759, *On the Contradictions of the World.*[13] Moreover, he quoted at length from the French author in *An Enquiry into the Present State of Polite Learning in Europe;*[14] he wrote for the newspaper, as a Chinese letter, an apostrophe on his supposed death,[15] and undertook the complimentary labor of composing his biography, which he filled with extravagant but well-placed praise. Innumerable references in Goldsmith's works indicate his esteem for Voltaire; and the careful reader will find that many opinions expressed are a repetition of ideas recorded in the works of that author; but these I cannot further notice here.[16]

Voltaire did not, like some writers who will be discussed later, furnish a model of his own composition for Goldsmith to imitate; but he exerted an even stronger influence upon the young author when he, speaking from his established position as a man of genius, pointed out the suitability of choosing a Chinese for the hero of his work, and drove home the realization of the rare possibilities of pseudo-letters for satirical writing. I have already suggested that an author who aspired only to popularity might at this time easily have found it by writing on the favorite topic of China; but Goldsmith had a less ephemeral purpose in mind. His foreign observer was to be the oracle who directed English destinies; such an oracle must of necessity be wise

---

[13] 2. 317, 340, 356, 410.
[14] 3. 504-6.
[15] *Public Ledger,* June 3, 1760. *The Citizen of the World,* Letter XLIII.
[16] See *Works,* Vol. 5, index, also especially 4. 20, note.

and dignified, if his opinions were to carry the weight of required authority, as formerly did those of the mysteriously learned Isaac Bickerstaff and the admired Spectator.

In the writings of Voltaire, Goldsmith found authoritative support of the learning, antiquity, and wisdom of the Chinese. In the passages of his *Mélanges,* in his article *Chine,* and in dozens of places, the French author filled his pages with comment on the genius of that nation, making comparisons even to the serious disadvantage of Occidental civilization. That Goldsmith was deep in the perusal of these passages will appear later; for the present let it suffice to say that his attention was called by Voltaire to the excellence of Chinese laws, morals, government, and social institutions. Having written ten of his works on Oriental subject-matters, Voltaire treated in his *Dictionnaire Philosophique, Histoire Universelle,* and his plays, the subject which in England was a social pastime—with all the seriousness of philosophic criticism.

More important even than Voltaire's serious comments on the wisdom of the East, were his remarks concerning the value of the pseudo-letter, to which he was the means of directing Goldsmith's consideration. The devices that had formerly been used in periodicals to attract attention, to hold interest, and to demand respect for the writer, had had their day. A Tatler or a Spectator would no longer do. New appeal was needed in fresh form. A learned foreign critic who exposed the English nation to unfavorable comparison with his own country offered so much novelty that it was certain of favor. Voltaire in his *Siècle de Louis XIV* pointed out to his readers that the gates of the French Academy had been opened to no less a man than Montesquieu, because he had handled satire of that sort skilfully:

> Montesquieu (Charles de Secondat, baron de la Brède et de), président au parlement de Bordeaux, né en 1689, donna à l'âge de trente-deux ans les *Lettres*

persanes, ouvrage de plaisanterie, plein de traits qui annoncent un esprit plus solide que son livre. C'est une imitation du *Siamois* de Dufresny[17] et de l'*Espion turc;* mais imitation qui fait voir comment ces originaux devaient être écrits. Ces ouvrages d'ordinaire ne réussissent qu'à la faveur de l'air étranger; on met avec succès dans la bouche d'un Asiatique la satire de notre pays, qui serait bien moins acceuillie dans la bouche d'un compatriote; ce qui est commun par soi-même devient alors singulier.[18] Le génie qui règne dans les *Lettres persanes* ouvrit au président de Montesquieu les portes de l'Académie française.[19]

Goldsmith included a translation of this extract from the *Siècle de Louis XIV* in a review of another of Voltaire's works, the *Histoire Universelle,* which he wrote for the *Monthly Review* in August, 1757, going out of his way to do so.[20] This indicates that what Voltaire said concerning the reason for Montesquieu's success was food for thought to the young writer who was just then trying to establish his reputation in Grub Street.

[17] *Amusements Sérieux et Comiques d'un Siamois,* 1707.
[18] Cf. Goldsmith's review of the *Letters from an Armenian in Ireland,* in *Monthly Review,* August, 1757, where similar remarks are made.
[19] Voltaire, *Siècle de Louis XIV,* ed. Garnier Frères, 14. 106-7.
[20] *Monthly Review,* Aug., 1757, p. 163. *Letter to the Authors of the Monthly Review:* 'Charles Montesquieu, President of the Parliament of Bourdeaux, born in 1689, published, at the age of thirty-two, his *Persian Letters,* a work of humour, abounding with strokes which testify a genius above the performance. It is written in imitation of the *Siamese Letters* of Du Freny, and of the *Turkish Spy;* but it is an imitation which shews what the originals should have been. The success their works met with was, for the most part, owing to the foreign air of their performances; the success of the *Persian Letters* arose from the delicacy of their satire. That satire which in the mouth of an Asiatic is poignant, would lose all its force when coming from an European. The genius which appeared in this performance opened to Mr. Montesquieu the gates of the French Academy.' Reprinted in *Works* 4. 281.

Further evidence that Voltaire influenced Goldsmith is contained in Goldsmith's criticism of another book of pseudo-epistles, *Letters from an Armenian in Ireland to his Friends at Trebisonde.* This article, in fact, appeared in the same issue of the *Monthly Review.* In it he makes a special point of Voltaire's statement that 'satire which in the mouth of an Asiatic is poignant, would lose all its force when coming from an European.' From this article it is apparent that his ideas about writings of this character were beginning to take shape under Voltaire's tutelage. On this point I shall have more to say later; first, there are other manifestations of his evolving plan which require mention.

In point of date, the next reference to the plan occurs in a letter which was written August 14, 1758, to his cousin, Robert Bryanton.[21] In this instance Goldsmith speaks of creating a Chinese character, but he does not specify the pseudo-letter form. He says: 'I shall soon make our Chinese talk like an Englishman,' and he refers to himself as 'the Confucius of Europe.' Undoubtedly he had in mind the Chinese letters. It has been pointed out by Prior, however, that Goldsmith did not at first intend to make the hero of that work a Chinese.[22] The biographer asserts that, according to reports of Goldsmith's friends, a native of Morocco or Fez was selected, as offering more novelty of character than a Turk or Persian; but confirmation of Prior's report cannot be found.

There is, perhaps, further indication in an article which Goldsmith wrote in May, 1759, that he had not yet fully determined upon the Chinese nationality of his philosophic wanderer. This indication is found in his comments on Arthur Murphy's the *Orphan of China,*[23] which ridicules the prevailing fad for Chinese literature and art. He speaks contemptuously of Chinese gardens, of houses ornamented

[21] Reprinted in *Works* I. 437.
[22] *Life of Goldsmith* I. 360.
[23] *Critical Review,* May, 1759.

in the front with zigzag lines, and of rooms crowded with Chinese vases and Indian pagodas. He said sneeringly that in such times even poetry might conform to Chinese taste. 'Of all nations that ever felt the influence of the inspiring goddess,' he continues, 'perhaps the Chinese are to be placed in the lowest class: their productions are the most phlegmatic that can be imagined. . . . There is not a single attempt to address the imagination, or influence the passions; such therefore are very improper models for imitation.'[24] Yet eight months later he made a Chinese the critic of the customs of England. Hack-writing and hack-criticism must not be taken too seriously.

In November, Goldsmith again turned to Voltaire, translating (as a contribution to the *Bee*[25]) that portion of his article, *Contradictions*, which dealt with pseudo-letters. Voltaire's essay had been printed twice; first, among the *Mélanges*, in the edition of *1742*, and later in the collected

---

[24] See *Works* 4. 350-1.

[25] The translation appeared in the *Bee*, Nov. 10, 1759, under the title 'On the Contradictions of the World.' It reads: 'Should an Asiatic come among us, what judgment could he form of our religion! Or would he not think that of Paganism still continued! The days of the week still retain the names of heathen deities, our churches are filled with statues of the gods of the ancients; and should he sometimes be a spectator at our theatres, he might mistake the scene for a temple to their honour, and our assiduity for devotion.

'In Spain, our Asiatic would be surprised to find severe laws, which forbid strangers carrying on any commerce to America; and yet he might see strangers alone in possession of that prohibited trade; and the Spaniards, in effect, no more than factors to others. whom they enrich, while they continue in poverty. How would he be surprised to find our actors styled vagabonds by law, yet encouraged by the great, and kept company with as equals! He would find the press loaded with works which every one condemns, and yet all are eager to purchase. He would everywhere find.our customs in opposition to our statutes. He might probably laugh at our absurdities; yet, should we take a voyage into Asia, we might see the same absurdities practised with very little variation.'—*Works* 2. 413.

works that appeared in 1756.[26]   The passage used reads in
the original:

> Un Asiatique qui voyagerait en Europe pourrait bien
> nous prendre pour des païens.   Nos jours de la semaine
> portent les noms de Mars, de Mercure, de Jupiter, de
> Vénus; les noces de Cupidon et de Psyché sont peintes
> dans la maison des papes; mais surtout si cet Asiatique
> voyait notre opéra, il ne douterait pas que ce ne fût une
> fête à l'honneur des dieux du paganisme.   S'il s'infor-
> mait un peu plus exactement de nos mœurs, il serait
> bien plus étonné; il verrait en Espagne qu'une loi
> sévère défend qu'aucun étranger ait la moindre part
> indirecte au commerce de l'Amérique, et que cependant
> les étrangers y font, par les facteurs espagnols, un
> commerce de cinquante millions par an, de sorte que
> l'Espagne ne peut s'enrichir que par la violation de la
> loi, toujours subsistante et toujours méprisée.   Il
> verrait qu'en un autre pays le gouvernement fait fleurir
> une compagnie des Indes, et que les théologiens ont
> déclaré le dividende des actions criminels devant Dieu.
> Il verrait qu'on achète le droit de juger les hommes,
> celui de commander à la guerre, celui d'entrer au
> conseil; il ne pourrait comprendre pourquoi il est dit
> dans les patentes qui donnent ces places, qu'elles ont
> été accordées gratis et sans brigue, tandis que la
> quittance de finance est attachée aux lettres de provi-
> sion.   Notre Asiatique ne serait-il pas surpris de voir
> des comédiens gagés par les souverains, et excom-
> muniés par les curés?   Il demanderait pourquoi un
> lieutenant général roturier, qui aura gagné des batailles,
> sera mis à la taille comme un paysan, et qu'un échevin
> sera noble comme les Montmorency?   Pourquoi, tandis

---

[26] Gibbs states (*Works* 3. 1) that 'Voltaire's "Asiatic" in *The
Philosophical Dictionary*' is a source of inspiration to Goldsmith.
'The Asiatic' did not appear in the *Dictionnaire Philosophique* until
1764, when the editors Kahl placed it there, three years after the
appearance of the *Chinese Letters*. Obviously Gibbs is in error.
The passages referred to are to be found in the article 'Contradictions,' 1742. Austin Dobson, undoubtedly following Gibbs, makes
the same mistake.

qu'on interdit les spectacles réguliers, dans une semaine consacrée à l'édification, on permet des bateleurs qui offensent les oreilles les moins délicates? Il verrait presque toujours nos usages en contradiction avec nos lois; et si nous voyagions en Asie, nous y trouverions à peu près les mêmes incompatibilités.[27]

It is interesting to note that Goldsmith later, in his *Chinese Letters*, makes use of the very points suggested by Voltaire, in his own satire. The following examples of French foibles are cited as suitable objects of criticism for an Asiatic traveling in Europe: (1) The continuance of superstitions in French life; (2) the illegitimate commerce carried on by Spain; (3) the mercenary system which allows men to buy positions of authority in which they can judge others; (4) the granting of patents avowedly gratis, with the sum of their cost attached; (5) the engagement of actors by sovereigns, and their excommunication by the clergy; (6) the depreciation of really great men, and the exaltation of worthless ones; (7) the forbidding of plays, and the tolerance of those which offend the least delicate taste.

Goldsmith's use of these suggestions is found in the following places: in the *Chinese Letters,* Letter XV, he points out the absurdities of believing the superstitions which are advanced by certain recent authors of note;[28] in Letter LXXXIV he treats the topic of actors, showing that 'though the law of this country holds them as vagabonds, many of them earn more than a thousand a year.'[29] Goldsmith paraphrased Voltaire's '. . . des comédiens gagés par les souverains, et excommuniés par les curés' in this way: 'Our actors styled vagabonds by law, yet encouraged by the

---

[27] Reprinted in *Œuvres de Voltaire,* ed. Garnier Frères, 18. 255.
[28] *Citizen of the World,* Letter XVI.
[29] *Citizen of the World,* Letter LXXXV.

great, and kept company with as equals.'[30] In Letter XII
he shows that men of no worth are often highly honored,
while real genius is neglected.[31] In Letter XX Goldsmith objects to the tolerance of worthless plays which
offend good taste.[32] So four of the five topics mentioned
by Voltaire, as suitable for the criticism of the Asiatic, are
actually used in the *Chinese Letters*.

That Goldsmith was, even as he wrote the review,
enlarging on the proposed plan of Voltaire, is indicated by
his including in his avowed translation a subject fit for the
satire of our Oriental of which the French author made no
mention. Goldsmith says 'He [the Asiatic] would find the
press loaded with works which every one condemns, and yet
all are eager to purchase.' Voltaire makes no such remark.
Goldsmith fitted it into his plan of the imaginary pseudo-
letter scheme. It is a clear indication that he was beginning
to amplify in his mind the suggestions made for this kind of
composition. The point here interpolated into Voltaire's
text receives exhaustive treatment in the *Chinese Letters*,
No. LI, where Goldsmith alludes specifically to the publication of *Tristram Shandy,* and other works.[33]

On October 6, 1759, Goldsmith began to put his theories
into practice by printing a pseudo-letter in the *Bee*, No. 1.
It is announced as 'A Letter from a Traveller,' was
supposedly written by a foreigner criticizing the land he
is visiting, and treated of the condition of the Poles. The
editor promised; 'The sequel of this correspondence to be
continued occasionally. I shall alter nothing either in style
or substance of these letters, and the reader may depend

[30] In *Works* 4. 413, note, Gibbs says, 'Voltaire's essay has not
this remark concerning actors. It is an interpolation of the translator
and applies to the English law.' The error of Gibbs' remark can be
seen by consulting Voltaire's text, quoted above. See above, p. 12.
[31] *Citizen of the World*, Letter XIII.
[32] *Citizen of the World*, Letter XXI.
[33] *Citizen of the World*, Letter LIII.

upon their being genuine.'[34] The letter is taken literally from Justus von Effen's *Relation d'un Voyage de Hollande en Suède,* printed in 1729 at the end of *Le Misanthrope.*[35] It is descriptive rather than satirical.

In the next number of the *Bee,* Goldsmith printed an account of the Swedes by a foreign visitor to their land. This letter is skilfully pieced together from the eighth and eleventh chapters of von Effen's *Relation.*[36] By these writings, published prior to *The Citizen of the World,* he tested the effectiveness of the pseudo-letter device.

The details of the larger venture, which he was now ready to undertake, had been over two years in maturing. After considerable pondering on the Chinese material, after considering and experimenting with the pseudo-letter, he joined them in the pages of the *Public Ledger* in serial form. The success of these essays justified a collected edition two years later, in 1762. The two volumes which contained them bore the striking title, *The Citizen of the World.*

CHAPTER II

THE VENTURE IN JOURNALISM.

The Chinese letters appeared at last, in the *Public Ledger,* a daily paper, professing to be a 'register of commerce and intelligence.' The initial number was printed on January 12, 1760. The project was John Newbery's (for whose *British Magazine* Goldsmith was at the time writing).[1] He chose either Griffith Jones or Hugh Kelly,

[34] See *Works* 2. 319, and notes 2 and 3.

[35] The authorship was discovered by A. J. Barnouw. See *Modern Language Review* 8. 319.

[36] *Bee,* Oct. 13, 1759: 'An Account of the Swedes, with some Particulars Relative to Charles XII.' See *Works* 2. 329.

[1] John Newbery (1713-67) was a publisher and originator of children's books. Among his literary clients were Dr. Johnson, Christopher Smart, Dr. Dodd, and Oliver Goldsmith.

the dramatist, as editor.[2]   Printed at Mr. Bristow's office, 'next the great toy-shop in St. Paul's church-yard,' the first number was circulated gratis, with the announcement that future copies would sell for twopence half-penny.[3]   It contained a considerable amount of shipping news, a few lines of parliamentary information, foreign notes, war news, and court anecdotes.

An advertisement in the first number sketched the policy of the paper: 'We are unwilling to raise expectations which we may perhaps find ourselves unable to satisfy: and there-fore have made no mention of criticism or literature, which yet we do not professedly exclude; nor shall we reject any political essays which are apparently calculated for the public good.[4]   The dullness of the first few numbers warranted a no less modest announcement.

Prior says that, according to contemporary statements, Goldsmith was secured by Newbery to contribute to the new paper two amusing articles a week, for which he received the payment of one hundred pounds a year, that is, about a guinea a paper.[5]   The first numbers of *The Ledger* were probably left to the supervision of Jones or Kelly, or perhaps of Newbery himself; and it is likely that Gold-smith's first article was the letter: 'To the Authors of *The Public Ledger*', in No. 5, on January 17, 1760.[6]   This letter vindicated the bravery and character of the French, and ridiculed the English habit of condemning everything foreign.   Goldsmith's next article appeared in No. 9, January

---

[2] Griffith Jones (1722-86), editor, as well, of the *London Chronicle* and the *Public Advertiser;* printed the *Literary* and the *British Magazine.*

Hugh Kelly (1739-77), playwright and author.

[3] The price is given in the *Public Ledger*, p. 1.

[4] *Public Ledger*, January 24. 1760.

[5] See *Life* 1. 356.

[6] Reprinted in *Works* 4. 468.

22,[7] and was headed: 'To The Ladies of London and West-minster, Greeting.'[8] In it the author, from his country estate, addresses 'the ladies' and praises 'the Goddess of Silence' as their friend. Both papers have charm of style, and characteristics of the author's manner. They are probably Goldsmith's only communications to the *Public Ledger* before the beginning of his series.

A third fugitive piece was written by Goldsmith, but after the Chinese-letters series was begun.[9] In 1760 Newbery began publishing in the *British Magazine;* Goldsmith and Smollett were among the chief contributors. In order to advertise the magazine with which he was affiliated, and to praise Smollett, Goldsmith published in the *Public Ledger,* February 16, 1760: 'The description of a Wow-Wow in the Country.' Referring in this article to Smollett's *Adventures of Sir Launcelot Greaves,* the author commented through one of his characters: ' "That piece, gentlemen," says he, " is written in the very spirit and manner of Cervantes; there is great knowledge of human nature, and evident marks of the master in almost every sentence; and from the plan, the humour, and the execution, I can venture to say that it dropt from the pen of the ingenious Dr. ——." Every one was pleased with the performance, and I was particularly gratified in hearing all the sensible part of the company give orders for the 'British Magazine.'[10] This curious piece of journalistic advertising is a specimen of the kind of hack-writing which Goldsmith, at this time, was willing to undertake.

---

[7] Both Prior and Forster state that this letter appeared in No. 7 of the *Public Ledger*. Gibbs states correctly that it appeared in No. 9, Jan. 22, 1760. See *Works* 4. 471, note. See also Prior's *Life* 1. 357.

[8] Reprinted in *Works* 4. 471.

[9] *Public Ledger*, February 16, 1760.

[10] Reprinted in *Works* 4. 476.

Although the canon of Goldsmith's writing in the *Public Ledger* is far from established, the three above-mentioned letters, and those of the Chinese series, almost made up his stated proportion of two a week. Prior says:[11] 'There is little doubt that he furnished others, though possibly less finished and more difficult to trace; such as on the encouragement to Opera Singers and Operas[12] (Sept. 16th), and on the Institution of Amateur Concerts for the benefit of the Poor, November 3d.'[13]

It may be assumed that the ambitious author had not at first made up his mind to risk his pseudo-letter scheme in a newborn journal which made so little pretense to merit, even by its own boast, and that, in writing two fugitive pieces, he was waiting to know the success of the untried journal, before risking in its pages his cherished series. He was, however, busily engaged in satisfying demands from the *British Magazine* and other periodicals; the *Public Ledger* was demanding two papers a week, and Goldsmith was in need of money. Perhaps these circumstances induced him to begin a series which he had definitely in mind, which with slight ingenuity could be suited to the mood of the moment, drawn from the nearest source-book, or suggested by casual observations.

At any rate, the first Chinese letter appeared on January 24, 1760. Addressed simply to 'Mr.*****, merchant in London,' it was printed on the first page, in the second column, but inconspicuously, without even the heading of 'Letter.' A reply to this letter immediately followed; and

---

[11] *Life* I. 361.

[12] An article appeared in the *Public Ledger,* Sept. 16, 1760, inveighing against Italian opera, and in favor of British opera. There is no title, but it is the first article, and is in a form of letter addressed 'To the Printer.'

[13] *Public Ledger,* Nov. 3, 1760. The article appeared without title, in the form of a letter addressed 'To the Printer.'

this was the first from the Chinese mandarin, Lien Chi Altangi.[14] The next two communications were likewise unnumbered, but, on February 1, the letter of Fum Hoam was 'Letter IV,' indicating, for the first time, a series. Gibbs observes that this lack of numbering seemed to indicate that a series was not at first intended.[15] In view of the fact that Goldsmith's scheme for the letters had been established previously, this could not, I think, have been his reason for leaving the earlier letters unnumbered. His purpose was rather to give the impression that the articles were casual communications from a Chinese visiting London. Having once aroused interest in his Oriental, the indication of a continued series served as an advertisement.

In January, 1760, three letters were published, in February ten, in March ten, in April eight, in May ten, in June eleven, in July eight, in August nine, in September ten, in October ten, in November six, and in December three, making a total of ninety-eight letters (not counting separately the brief introductory letter of January 24, 1760). The newspaper numbering was ninety-seven. This error arose from Goldsmith's numbering two consecutive papers XLVIII.[16] So during the year 1760, until November, there was apparently no falling off in the public demand for Lien's philosophic observations; for an average of ten a month was maintained.

The decrease of six letters in November, and three in December, was due partly to Goldsmith's increased activities in other directions, partly, perhaps, to lack of public enthusiasm. He resumed at this time his connection with the *Ladies' Magazine,* acting as editor or contributor. His

[14] This letter is unnumbered in the *Public Ledger,* and is Letter II in *The Citizen of the World.*

[15] See *Works* 3. 13, note.

[16] Prior (*Life* 1. 361) errs in saying that it was No. XXV which was twice used.

work increased steadily from November, 1760, until April, when the issue was almost entirely of his own composition.[17] At the same time he was engaged in other hack-work.

In the following year, 1761, there was a marked falling-off in the number of Chinese letters. In January six letters were published, in February three, in March three, in April three, in May three, in June none, while in July and August, respectively, only one letter appeared.[18] On the fourteenth of this last month the series was brought to a close. There had been in all one hundred and eighteen letters.

These statistics indicate a considerable popularity for Goldsmith's venture, especially in the year 1760. Newbery, an experienced publisher, looked to it to forward the sale of his newspaper; and, according to Prior, it not only enlarged the circulation, but also laid the foundation of its permanency.[19] He adds that the lucubrations of the foreign philosopher were generally read and admired, and that they furnished Goldsmith his just assurance of literary success.

Such statements are supported by fact. The third paper on January 31 was placed in the first column. After this, letters IV, VI, X, and XIV appeared as second and third-column articles, but always on the first page. After the issue of the *Public Ledger* dated March 11, 1760, all subsequent letters were in the first column, in the important position of 'leaders.'

The republication of these letters in current periodicals was proof of their popularity. The *Royal Magazine* reprinted in January, with few changes of text (except in the opening paragraphs), Goldsmith's Chinese letter of January 9. The *Court Miscellany* reprinted in March, 1766, the story of Choang and Hansi, which had appeared in the *Public Ledger* on March 15, 1760. The *British*

[17] Prior, *Life* 1. 364-5.
[18] See tabulated list in Appendix, p. 125.
[19] *Life* 1. 362.

Magazine, in July, 1760, repeated the Chinese letter of January 18, 1760; in August, 1760, that of August 19, 1760; in September, 1760, that of September 12, 1760; in December, 1760, that of December 17, 1760; in March, 1761, that of March 18, 1761.

In September, 1761, the *Gentleman's Magazine* printed an article entitled: 'The Folly of Keeping, *what is called,* the best company,' signed Laurence Grogan. This was a clever parody of Goldsmith's essays on Beau Tibbs (*Public Ledger,* July 2, 1760; August 1, 1760; September 2, 1760; and December 29, 1760). The names of the characters were altered, the favorite combination of names, 'Carolina Wilhelmina Amelia' (so often used in different forms by Goldsmith), was once more varied, the snobbery of the Little Beau parodied, and Goldsmith's characteristic method of closing mimicked. Such republications and parodies indicate the extent to which the Chinese letters were known.

If the author of the Chinese letters had reason to be pleased with their instant popularity, he also had reason to be disappointed at the partial failure of the purpose for which they had been designed. It was his aim to conceal his identity, and to hide behind the guise of a mandarin sending communications to a London paper. Undoubtedly Goldsmith believed that the effectiveness of his satire depended upon the acceptance of his Chinese hero by the public.

He did not plan that his foreign observer should be a mere geographer. 'Let European travellers cross seas and deserts merely to measure the height of a mountain, to describe the cataract of a river, or tell the commodities which every country can produce.'[20] Goldsmith intended that his traveler should study the human heart, know the *men* of every country, and discover the differences which resulted

---

[20] *The Citizen of the World,* ed. Gibbs, 3. 32. See entire letter VII.

from climate, religion, education, prejudice, and partiality.[21]
His purpose was further, through him, to disclose the morals
and opinions of the English; to expose their political
intrigues, and to show their skill in sciences. It was not
so much his intention to characterize a people in general
terms as to give in detail the minute circumstances which
influenced their opinions.[22] It was not his purpose to
satisfy curiosity, but, by exposing the foibles of the
English, to teach them wisdom.

A lighter side aimed simply at amusement through
narrative, not only by making the hero fall frequently into
story-telling, but also, by means of a frame-tale embracing
the whole, the author aimed to supply this interest.[23] The
story is briefly: By leaving China without permission, Lien
the philosopher angered the emperor. His money and
estate were confiscated, his wife cast into prison, and his
son narrowly saved from the same fate, through the aid of
a faithful friend. This son, Hingpo, fled from China,
and had various adventures in Persia. There he saved
Zelis, a beautiful Christian captive, from the harem of
Mostodad, and fled with her into Russia. Here they were
attacked by pirates, and separated. Zelis turned out in the
end to be the niece of the Man-in-Black, the Chinese philosopher's constant companion and guide in London. When
Hingpo joined his father in that city, he met with his beloved,
who had arrived safely from Russia, and a happy conclusion
followed.

Into such a narrative the acquaintances of Lien were
easily introduced, and finally were disposed of at the
wedding dinner of the young couple. The details of

---

[21] *Ibid.* 3. 25.

[22] *Ibid.* 3. 127.

[23] The frame-tale is found in the following letters of *The Citizen
of the World:* Nos. VI, XXII, XXXV, XXXVI, XXXVII, XLVII,
LIX, LX, LXI, XCIV, CXXIII. All of it appeared in the *Public
Ledger* version.

Hingpo's sufferings were given in letters written by the son to the father; while the father's consoling replies afforded excellent opportunity for Goldsmith to show his erudition, by the means of maxims of Confucius. Narrative of this sort could be continued until the author saw the popularity of his letters declining, at which period the conclusion, as a loosely connected tale, formed an effective close to the entire series.

Goldsmith, though he had exercised all his ingenuity in trying to enforce the deception, failed to convince the public that a Chinese was the author of these contributions to the *Public Ledger*.

By the frequent use of Chinese names, by many references to Chinese geography, citations of Chinese proverbs, quotation of the maxims of Confucius, relating of anecdotes about Chinese sovereigns, mention of Eastern festivals, the details of Chinese life, habits, and opinions, and references to himself as a native of China, the narrator of the pseudo-letters had expected to establish belief in his pretended nationality. For example, on March 24, 1760, Goldsmith wrote this footnote: 'This whole apostrophe seems most literally translated from Ambulaaohamed, the Arabian poet.'[24] There was no such Arabian poet, and the apostrophe bore no resemblance to Arabian style. Such pretense was transparent, and the *Public Ledger* soon began receiving letters which aimed to expose the deception.

Many of the correspondents apparently attacked him on stylistic grounds. The pseudo-Oriental works of the period were written in an extravagant, lofty style, which in no way resembled their originals, but which was popularly conceded to be the Eastern manner. Goldsmith, with considerable justice, defended his simpler diction. In one place he quoted an Englishman, whom he took to be an author:

[24] Letter XXI in the *Public Ledger; The Citizen of the World*, Letter XXII.

'Eastern tales should always be sonorous, lofty, musical, and unmeaning';[25] in another, Goldsmith said that the reviewers of Oriental tales believed that in true Eastern style 'nought else is required but sublimity. . . . All is great, obscure, magnificent, and unintelligible.'[26] His Chinese philosopher contradicted such statements by saying: 'What is palmed off . . . daily for an imitation of Eastern writing, no way resembles their manner, either in sentiment or diction.'[27] The credence in such replies was enforced by continual reference to the speaker's nationality, as 'Take, Sir, the word of one who is *professedly* a Chinese, and who is *actually* acquainted with Arabian writers';[28] and again: 'I could not avoid smiling to hear a native of England attempt to instruct me in the true eastern idiom.'[29]

These were efforts to induce a belief in the philosopher's nationality. When Goldsmith saw his style criticized, realizing that he had fallen too much into the English manner, he attempted to cover up and explain his fault by printing as heading to the *Letter* of May 2, 1760: 'The editor on this, and every other occasion, has endeavoured to translate the letter-writer in such a manner as he himself, had he perfectly understood English, would have written.'[30]

Goldsmith sometimes attempted to cover up the transparency of his deception by exposing the English ignorance, not only of Eastern rhetoric, but also of Eastern customs in general. For example, he devoted the letter of April 25, 1760, to instructing a lady of distinction in the practical use of Oriental *knickknacks,* which she had considered

[25] *Public Ledger,* Letter XXXI, April 25, 1760. *The Citizen of the World,* Letter XXXIII.

[26] *Public Ledger,* No. XXXI. *The Citizen of the World,* Letter XXXIII, reads: 'Nothing more is required but sublimity.'

[27] *Ibid.*

[28] *Public Ledger,* Letter XXXI, April 25, 1760.

[29] *Ibid.*

[30] *Public Ledger,* Letter XXXII.

'perfectly beautiful, and perfectly useless.'[31] He later taught her the facts of the Chinese manner of eating, and of other Chinese customs. Her false conceptions of the Chinese in these particulars were due to 'the fictions propagated here, under the titles of Eastern tales and Oriental histories.'

When Goldsmith realized that the public refused to believe that a Chinese had written the letters, he began to drop the pretense. In the early numbers of the series the letters of February 4, February 28, and April 25[32] were filled with writing which aimed to establish the nationality of his Chinese, but after the first three months, the Oriental setting grew thinner as the series advanced, footnotes acknowledged the sources of his Oriental erudition,[33] and the real Goldsmith wrote in his best vein, as satirist, as the creator of the inimitable Beau Tibbs, as an English essayist, unhampered by any restricting pretense. When he returned to the Chinese vein, it was not to continue the deception, but to carry out the scheme of pseudo-letters.

CHAPTER III

THE CITIZEN OF THE WORLD.

Two small duodecimo volumes, entitled *The Citizen of the World; or Letters from a Chinese Philosopher, Residing in London, to his Friends in the East,* appeared on May 1, 1762. They contained the Chinese letters republished, and were a belated answer to a promise in a note after the concluding letter of the newspaper series. This read: 'It may not be improper to inform the Public that these letters

---

[31] *Public Ledger,* Letter XXXI.
[32] *Public Ledger,* Letters V, XIII, XXXI.
[33] See especially *Public Ledger,* Letters LXVII, LXXXII, and LXXXVII. These letters are, in *The Citizen of the World,* numbered LXVIII, LXXXIII, and XCV.

will shortly be published, in two Volumes of the usual Spectator Size. The numerous Errors of the Press are corrected, and the Errors of the Writer, still, perhaps, more numerous, are retrenched. Some new Letters are added, and others, which were remarkable only for being dull, are wholly omitted. In short, such Pains have been taken, that the Editor will, perhaps, receive more Praise for his Industry, than the Writer for his Genius. I could be prolix upon the present Occasion, but shall be silent, for when we talk of ourselves, Vanity, or Resentment have always too much to say.'[1]

In the collected edition numerous corrections were made, a considerable amount of revision was undertaken, and the order of the essays changed, so as to bring together those on the same or similar subjects. Goldsmith, however, omitted no essay which had originally appeared in the *Public Ledger;* but in the second particular he kept his word, and added four essays. Two of these were written especially for the new edition.[2] The other two had appeared previously. Letter CXVII, 'A City Night Piece,' was taken from the *Bee,* Saturday, October 27, 1759; Letter CXIX, 'The Distresses of a Common Soldier,' from the *British Magazine,* June, 1760.

There were in all one hundred and eighteen letters in the original series; while in *The Citizen of the World* there were one hundred and twenty-three letters. The last letter in the early bound editions was numbered CXIX. The error occurred from a misnumbering, similar to that in the *Public Ledger.* In the present case, numbers XXV, XLVII and CXVI were used twice for the same articles.

These new volumes, like the original letters, appeared anonymously, the author merely acknowledging translation; otherwise the whole underlying scheme would have been

---

[1] Following Letter CXVI in the *Public Ledger.*
[2] Letters CXXI and CXXII.

removed. They were 'Printed for the author,' which, as Prior says, was 'the only intimation of the kind attached to Goldsmith's works.'[3] Advertised by J. Newbery and W. Bristow, in St. Paul's Churchyard, they sold for six shillings,[4] and are said to have brought the author a total sum of ten to fifteen pounds.[5]

At first, it appeared, there was some hesitancy on Newbery's part to assume the responsibility of reprinting a work which had amply satisfied his purpose in the *Public Ledger*. Prior says that he may even have declined the offer of publication. A note of hand, however, shows either that the original publisher ultimately decided in favor of acceptance, or, as the new title was not used, paid up an outstanding account. It read: 'Received of Mr. Newbery five guineas, which, with what I have received at different times before, is in full for the copy of Chinese Letters, as witness my hand. Oliver Goldsmith. March 5, 1762.'[6]

But the new volumes did appear; they bore the title, *The Citizen of the World*. That so happy a phrase was chosen to launch the bound edition of the *Chinese Letters* is significant of the genius of their author. Goldsmith realized the importance of titles. It is said of him that on the occasion of a visit to Isaac Taylor, a well known engraver, his host consulted him upon the title of a book, with an apology for troubling him with so trifling a matter, to which Goldsmith rejoined with emphasis, 'The title, sir; why the title is everything.'[7] And in selecting titles for his own works, Goldsmith used the greatest care. *The Bee* is a suggestive name for an active periodical; *She Stoops to*

---

[3] *Life* I. 396.

[4] The price of the volumes was announced in the notices of the various magazines. See *Monthly Review*, June, 1762, p. 477.

[5] Prior's *Life* I. 417.

[6] *Ibid.* I. 397.

[7] *Memorials of Mrs. Gilbert*, 1874.

Conquer is a succinctly descriptive title for a diverting comedy. Yet if Goldsmith was careful to find the most appropriate titles for his writings, he was willing enough not to be the originator of them. The title of the *Bee* was probably borrowed from either James Anderson's or Eustace Budgell's periodicals of the same name; the phrase, *She Stoops to Conquer,* is from Dryden; while the phrase, *The Citizen of the World,* may be found in a variety of places.

Goldsmith used the phrase 'the Citizen of the World' for the first time in the *Memoirs of M. Voltaire,* where he comments: 'When she was gone, those ties which held him to his country were broken, and he considered himself, in every sense of the word, a citizen of the world.'[8] The first appearance of the phrase in the *Public Ledger* is in the issue of March 20, 1760.[9] Here it occurs in the following context: 'Confucius observes that it is the duty of the learned to unite society more closely, and to persuade men to become citizens of the world.' Five days later, on March 25, 1760,[10] it appears as follows: 'I am particularly struck with one who writes these words upon the paper that enclosed his benefaction. *The Mite of an Englishman, a citizen of the world, to Frenchmen, prisoners of war, and naked.* In writing for the *British Magazine,* in August, 1760, in an essay 'On National Prejudices'[11] Goldsmith says:

> Among all the famous sayings of antiquity, there is none that does greater honour to the author, or affords greater pleasure to the reader, (at least if he be a person of a generous and benevolent heart) than that of the philosopher, who, being asked what *countryman* he was, replied, that he was a *citizen of the world.* . . . We are now become so much Englishmen,

---

[8] *Works* 4. 41.
[9] *Public Ledger,* Letter XIX, March 20, 1760.
[10] *Public Ledger,* Letter XXII, March 25, 1760.
[11] Reprinted in *Works* 1. 320-323.

Frenchmen, Dutchmen, Spaniards, or Germans, that we are no longer citizens of the world.[12]

Again in this same letter Goldsmith uses the phrase:

I should prefer the title of the antient philosopher, *viz*, a citizen of the world, to that of an Englishman, a Frenchman, an European, or to any other appellation whatever.[13]

Only in the above-mentioned places does Goldsmith use the phrase.

But the idea was not original with Goldsmith. Among the classic writers who made use of it were Socrates, Cicero, Lucian, Seneca, and Diogenes Laertius. Plutarch reports Socrates as saying, 'I am not of Athens, nor of Greece, but of the world.' The earliest use of it, however, as a single word, occurs in the philosopher Diogenes Laertius. It is very possible that Goldsmith was attracted to it in the classic authors; yet, as it was not forgotten in later days— for it recurred from time to time in the pages of modern writers—Goldsmith may have taken it from a more recent source. The source from which he borrowed it cannot be determined.[14] The importance, however, of the phrase does not lie in its previous use, but in its appropriate application to the bound volume which bore it as a title.

[12] *British Magazine,* August, 1760, p. 461.

[13] *Ibid.,* p. 462.

[14] The phrase, 'citizen of the world,' occurs in at least the following places before it was used by Goldsmith:

Socrates (see Plutarch).

B. C. 52 or 51, Cicero. *De Legibus* I. 161: 'civem totius mundi, quasi unius urbis.'

B. C. 45. Cicero, *Tusc. Disp.* 5. 108: 'Socrates quidem quum rogaretur, *cuiatem* se esse diceret, "Mundanum," inquit; totius enim mundi se incolam et civem arbitrabatur.'

A. D. ca. 50-60. Seneca, *Ep.* 120. 12 (of perfect man) 'Civem esse se universi et militem credens.'

A. D. ca. 80. Plutarch, *Of Exile,* p. 393: 'And yet Socrates said

Although the public had received the letters of Lien Chi
Altangi with enthusiasm when they were first printed as
Chinese Letters, it took little interest in their reappearance

better than so; who gave it out that he was neither Athenian nor
Grecian, but a citizen of the world.'

2d century.   Lucian, *Sale of Creeds* 8: (Diogenes speaks), 'It
means that I am a citizen of the world.'

3d century.   Diogenes Laertius seems to be the first to use
κοσμοπολίτης as a single word.

1304.   Dante, *De Vulgari Eloquentia* I. 6: 'Nos autem, cui
mundus est partia, velut piscibus æquor.'

1474.   Caxton, *Chesse* 31: 'Helde hym bourgeys, and cytezeyn of
the world.'

Before 1624.   Lord Herbert of Cherbury, *Autobiography*
(published by H. Walpole, 1764) : 'My intention in learning languages
being to make myself *a citizen of the world* as far as possible. . .'

1625.   Francis Bacon, *Of Goodness, and Goodness of Nature:* 'If
a man be gracious and courteous to strangers, it shews he is a *citizen
of the world,* and that his heart is no island cut off from other lands,
but a continent that joins to them.'

1647.   John Cleveland, *Satire on the Scots:*

> They live as rovers and defy
> This or that place, rags of geography,
> They'r *citizens o' th' world,* they'r all in all
> Scotland's a nation epidemical.

1700.   Puckle, *England's Path to Wealth and Honour:* 'An
honest man is a *citizen of the world.* Gain equalizeth all places to
me.'

1711.   Addison, *Spectator* 69. 'I am a Dane, Swede, or
Frenchman at different times; or rather fancy myself like the old
philosopher, who, upon being asked what countryman he was, replied,
that he was a *citizen of the world.*'

1721.   Montesquieu, *Letters Persanes,* Lettre LXVII, 'Le coeur
est citoyen de tous les pays.'

1750.   Fougeret de Monbron, *Le Cosmopolite.* Title reprinted
in 1752 under the title, *Citoyen du Monde.*

1752.   Lord Hyde, *Letter to David Mallet* (*Works of
Oliver Goldsmith,* ed. Gibbs, 4. 229). 'I owe to the regard which
he [Bolingbroke] has sometimes expressed for me, to disclaim it
rather privately to you, sir, who are instructed with his writings, and
to recommend to you to suppress that part of his work, (as a good

as *The Citizen of the World.*　As Prior says: 'No intimation of a second impression appears so late as May 1766,
when the name of the author, then rendered popular by the
success of the Traveller, was used in order to dispose of the
first.'　The second edition did not appear until 1769.
Prior falsely adds that a third edition did not come out until
about 1780;[15] the correct date of its appearance is 1774;
and this was the last edition to appear during Goldsmith's
lifetime.　Between 1774 and 1800 three English editions of
The Citizen of the World were printed.[16]

In France, *Le Citoyen du Monde* was more popular.
Montesquieu's great work had created an enormous interest
in pseudo-letters.　The whole device was, perhaps, better
suited to the French temperament.　The French translation of the *Citizen,* by M. Poire, published in 1763, went
through three editions.　In the next three years public
demand required four more editions of it.

The current contemporary reviews showed the unflattering
reception of *The Citizen of the World* by the English.
Many magazines passed by its publication without notice.
Among these was the best known monthly of the time,
the *Gentleman's Magazine.*　Others, which gave considerable space to the review of *the best books,* printed only a
notice of its appearance.　This was the sole acknowledgment by the *Universal Magazine,* the *London Magazine,*
the *Royal Magazine,* and the *Scots Magazine.*

The *British Magazine,* which had reprinted so many
Chinese letters from the *Public Ledger,* and to which
Goldsmith himself contributed, mentioned the reprinted
volumes by saying: 'Light, agreeable summer reading,

---

citizen of the World) for the world's peace and . . . not to raise
storms to his memory.'

1761. 'The address of a *citizen of the world,* to all the Princes
now in arms, to put a stop to the present destructive war.' 8vo,
pp. 59. The Hague.

[15] *Life* I. 401.

[16] 1792, 1793, 1799.

partly original, partly borrowed.' The *London Chronicle,* in May, 1766, announced: 'The greater part of this work was written by Dr. Goldsmith.'

Two magazines, the *Monthly Review,* and the *Critical Review,* contained longer accounts of *The Citizen of the World.* The former commented in June 1762:[17]

> Although this Chinese Philosopher has nothing Asiatic about him, and is as errant an European as the Philosopher of Malmesbury; yet he has some excellent remarks upon men, manners, and things—as the phrase goes.—But the Public have been already made sufficiently acquainted with the merit of these entertaining Letters, which were first printed in *The Ledger;* and are supposed to have contributed not a little towards the success of that Paper. They are said to be the work of the lively and ingenious Writer of An Enquiry into the present State of Polite Learning in Europe; a Writer, whom, it seems, we undesignedly offended, by some Strictures on the conduct of many of our modern Scribblers. As the observation was entirely general, in its intention, we were surprized to hear that this Gentleman had imagined himself in any degree pointed at, as we conceive nothing can be more illiberal in a Writer, or more foreign to the character of a Literary Journal, than to descend to the meanness of personal reflection. It is hoped that a charge of this sort can never be justly brought against the Monthly Review.

The account in the *Critical Review,* May, 1762, was still longer, but less appreciative. It ran:

> The remarkers upon human nature multiply so fast, that all the variety, inconsistency, and contradiction of human action, scarce furnish room for new observations. Every passion, appetite, and minute spring of conduct, hath been so accurately described, that nothing more remains for men of genius than to produce new combinations of old thoughts, instead of original ideas. To an extensive reader, the only novelty that appears in any recent publication, consists in the neatness of

[17] P. 477.

expression, the peculiar application of a trite reflection, and the perspicuity of arrangement; subtract the original sentiment from a folio volume, and it may be comprized in a six-penny pamphlet. The fault is not in the artists, but in the subject, which confines genius to mere modification. Human nature is now as stale a topic as the memory of an academician, which admits only of the same panegyric strewed over the ashes of twenty others of the fraternity.

Were we to examine these reflections of *our Citizen of the World* by the standard of originality, our pleasure would be greatly diminished; but let us view them with regard to utility, and we must confess their merit. What seem cloying to an hundred persons of fastidious appetites, may prove wholesome delicious nourishment to thousands. These letters, if we mistake not, made their first appearance in a daily news-paper, and were necessarily calculated to the meridian of the multitude, although they greatly surpass any late publications of the same nature, both in diction and sentiment. This circumstance alone would sufficiently plead the author's excuse, had he need of an apology; that genius must be fruitful, indeed, which can supply such a variety of tastes with daily entertainment. It is rather extraordinary, that the philosophic *Lien Chi Altangi* could handle so many topics agreeably, and sustain the fatigue of so long a course without weariness, than that he has sometimes stumbled. All his observations are marked with good sense, genius frequently breaks the fetters of restraint, and humour is sometimes successfully employed to enforce the dictates of reason. For a specimen of this last talent, we shall beg leave to transcribe the following imitation of a gazette, not as the best extract we could make to our purpose, but the shortest that now occurs. . . .

In the course of this correspondence between *Lien Chi* and his friends, we meet with a great number of ingenious criticisms upon men and books, which it would be needless to specify, as we most heartily recommend the whole performance to the perusal of our readers.[18]

---

[18] Pp. 397-400.

So *The Citizen of the World,* in bound volumes, made little stir in the literary world. Most of the magazines contained mere announcements of it. It was reviewed at length rather unflatteringly by two of the leading periodicals devoted solely to criticism. The work sold poorly; there were perhaps only two editions of it during the author's lifetime; and, after the publication of the first of these, the author did not find it worth his while to make many revisions of text.

The success of the Chinese letters, on the other hand, as periodical literature, had been marked. They established the reputation of the paper in which they were printed; they were the leading articles; they were discussed, copied, parodied. And they established Goldsmith's reputation as a writer. His cherished scheme did indeed result in producing the most noteworthy example of journalistic writing in the latter half of the century.

CHAPTER IV

THE PSEUDO-LETTER *Genre.*

The genre of pseudo-letters reached the point of highest merit in France with the *Lettres Persanes* of Montesquieu, and in England with *The Citizen of the World* of Goldsmith. But before the appearance of those two works, domestic criticism in a series of letters, by a pretended foreigner, was a well developed literary device. Voltaire pointed out the relation of the *Lettres Persanes* and the *Espion Turc* of Marana, which was first written in Italian in 1684, and in 1686 was translated into French and published at Paris.[1] Each subsequent edition added considerable material to the preceding one, and it is apparent that at least one-third of the completed work cannot be attributed to Marana, but is probably from the pen of Cotolendi, the author of *Mlle. de*

[1] See above, p. 7 ff.

Tournon.[2] Montesquieu not only found general inspiration in the work of the Spanish author, but also took from him specific details which he later put to use. Another writer who imitated Marana in this respect was Du Fresny, who in his *Amusements Sérieux et Comiques* posed, in order to examine French conditions with critical eyes, as a Siamese traveler at Paris.[3]

Both Montesquieu and Du Fresny copied Marana, who seems to deserve the credit of being the originator of the device in its developed form. Robert Boyle, however, in 1665 published his *Occasional Reflections,* which although not a collection of pseudo-letters, is a work in which effective but veiled satire is brought to bear on English conditions, through the remarks of intelligent but imaginary foreigners.[4]

The origin of the pseudo-letter type of satire can, perhaps, be found even further back. Toldo mentions as Marana's source the *Ragguagli di Parnaso* of Traiano Boccalini (1556-1613).

In this work the author, supposedly attending the meetings of Apollo, acts as story-teller and judge, much in the manner of Marana's Turkish Spy at Paris. Several writers have mentioned the possibility of the relationship between the *Ragguagli di Parnaso* and the *Espion Turc,* but there is no proof of it, and the suggestion merely points out an interesting analogy.[5]

---

[2] For a discussion of the authorship of the *Espion Turc,* see Toldo, 'Dell Espion Di Giovanni Paolo Marana e della sue attinenze con Le Lettres Persanes Del Montesquieu, in *Giornale Storico della Letteratura Italiana,'* 1897, 29. 46-79. Also see below, p. 39, note 2.

[3] See below, p. 136.

[4] See below, p. 133.

[5] Miss Conant has commented on the 'striking analogy' between these works, and cites, besides Toldo, the following writer who has pointed out the parallel: 'Antonio Belloni, in Vol. VII of *Storia Litteraria d' Italia . . . Il Seicento. . . . Milano,* 1898-1899, p. 374.' See Conant's *Oriental Tale in England,* p. 240, and note 1.

That Boccalini's scheme was suggested in a general way by Caporiali, in his poems, *Il Viaggio di Parnaso* and *Gli Avvisi di Parnaso,* is probable.[6] This again is speculation, for which there is little definite basis of fact.

And if one carries on mere speculation, there is reason to believe that the device of the *Espion Turc* grew out of sources much earlier than any of those just mentioned. The idea might conceivably have been borrowed from the dialogue of Lucian, in which the Scythian Anacharsis is represented as receiving from Solon the Athenian education.[7] Not only Athenian training, but Athenian customs and thought, are explained to Anacharsis, who sometimes compares them with his native ways, and sees them with Scythian eyes.

At any rate, the completed scheme of Montesquieu's *Lettres Persanes* had a gradual evolution, whether conscious or not, through the indicated gradations, from the simple dialogue of a native of a country explaining to a foreigner the customs of his land, until it appeared as it did in Montesquieu, a continued series of satiric letters with a much broader scope.

The citation of these examples does not aim to be inclusive, or even to establish the books mentioned in their proper relations. There were, indeed, many other parallel works, among them *L'Espion à Frankfort* (1741), *L'Espion Chinois en Europe* (1745), and *Les Lettres d'une Peruvienne*[8] by Mme. de Graffigny, in France; as well as the *Persian Letters*[9] by Lyttelton, and numerous isolated periodical articles, in England. These books will be discussed later as possible sources of Goldsmith's *The Citizen of the World.*

[6] Cf. *Giornale Storico,* 1887, 29. 46-79.
[7] Lucian, *Works,* ed. Fowler, 3. 191-212: *Anacharsis, A Discussion of Physical Training.*
[8] See below, p. 146.
[9] See above, p. 52.

A few of the possible sources of *The Citizen of the World* were known to the early biographers and editors of Goldsmith. Later commentators have been, for the most part, content to repeat what Prior and Forster said concerning the sources of Lien Chi Altangi's letters. Some have added a name or two to the specimens of the *genre,* but have seldom spoken concretely of what Goldsmith borrowed. Referring to the plan of *The Citizen of the World,* Prior says:[10]

> The idea was not new: The Turkish Spy, and the Persian and Peruvian Letters, and similar productions, had sought and secured much public attention in France. Swift had formed some such design, though not wholly the same, from the greater rudeness of the people who were to be introduced as giving the fruits of their observation, in making the Indian chiefs who were in London during the reign of Queen Anne tell the story of their travels; a project which by communicating to Steele, the latter marred by a paper or two in the 'Tatler' and 'Spectator.'

Forster says less on the subject. He remarks[11] that the first of the *Chinese Letters* 'threw out the hint of a series of letters, and of a kind of narrative as in the *Lettres Persanes,* and those pages of *The Spectator* which Swift suggested to Steele.' Cunningham adds to the list of works which are possible sources of the *Chinese Letters*: Defoe's *Tour Through England,* and Walpole's *Letter from Xo-Ho, a Chinese Philosopher at London, to his friend Lien Chi at Pekin.* He further points out the quotation from Voltaire made by Goldsmith in the *Monthly Review* for August, 1757, as a likely source of inspiration.[12] Austin Dobson adds one more to the list—*Les Lettres Chinoises,* by the

---

[10] *Life* I. 358-9.
[11] *Life and Times of Oliver Goldsmith* I. 252.
[12] Goldsmith's *Works,* ed. Cunningham, 2. 76.

Marquis D'Argens.[13] Dobson was also aware that Goldsmith adapted from Le Comte and Du Halde, but he considered these adaptations no longer important, failing to see their manifold significance with respect to Goldsmith's literary method.[14] J. W. M. Gibbs, the most recent and the best of Goldsmith's editors, adds nothing to the list of sources. Besides the above-mentioned writers, there are others who have commented in passing on the sources of *The Citizen of the World,* and perhaps cited a few details of similarity to Goldsmith's writing. Due acknowledgment of such cases will be made in the discussion of the individual source-books.

Examination of the books mentioned by commentators shows that they have listed, as possible sources of Goldsmith's letters, books which contain a plan closely similar to that of *The Citizen of the World*. The present writer thinks it wiser to confine discussion of sources to those writings for which there is conclusive evidence of contribution. Only books of this character, I think, can properly be so designated. Works of the other sort are of interest in relation to the history of the pseudo-letter *genre,* rather than in the relation to Goldsmith. However, since Goldsmith may have known them and read them, and they so far concern the question under discussion, they are listed in an appendix, where their presence in that section is explained. The books here considered as sources of the Chinese letters, then, are of two sorts : those which, having the same general plan, served Goldsmith concretely; and those which, without the plan, contributed definite material for his use. These two classes are treated separately in the chapters following.

---

[13] Prior knew this work, but did not mention it as a possible source.
[14] *The Citizen of the World*, ed. Dobson, Introduction.

CHAPTER V

THE SOURCES: GROUP A.

Works in which a foreigner is pictured satirizing the country he visits in a series of letters, made public in alleged translation from the original tongue.

1. 1687. MARANA, GIOVANNI PAOLO. *Letters writ by a Turkish Spy, who liv'd five and forty years ... at Paris: giving an Account ... of the most remarkable transactions of Europe ... from 1637 to 1682* (tr. from the French, by W. Bradshaw, and edited by Robert Midgley, M.D.). 8 vols., London, 1687-1693.[1]

Satire of the Occident by a disguised Oriental, writing a series of letters to the East, received its first great impetus from Giovanni Paolo Marana.[2] The preface to his *Turkish Spy* announces the discovery of a roll of manuscript, written by a Turkish spy, who comments on the social, political, and moral aspects of France for the extended

[1] The first French edition of *L'Espion Turc* appeared in 1686 at Paris and Amsterdam.

I have read Goldsmith's text with both the English translation and Marana's original. The translation is here referred to since: (1) Goldsmith was probably (or had recently been) reading the *Turkish Spy* when he referred to it in a letter to his uncle Contarine, May 8, 1753; an edition of the English translation had just appeared. (2) Goldsmith, however conversant with French, would probably have read eight bulky volumes in English. (3) There are no significant differences between the original and the translation; therefore, for the convenience of the reader, the English version is cited.

[2] Marana's authorship of the *Espion Turc* has been disputed by Henry Hallam. See Hallam's *Literature of Europe*, ed. 1837, 4. 554-8. J. M. Rigg refutes Hallam's opinion in the *Dict. Nat. Biog.* 13. 366-7.

number of years during which he acted as a spy at Paris. By pretending to translate and edit this manuscript, Marana hoped to conceal the Occidental authorship of his work. In the guise of the spy, he wrote hundreds of letters to friends in the East, while his friends replied as voluminously. The letters are, for the most part, satiric. They deal with European society; they ramble through hundreds of pages on current politics; and they contrast the morals of the East and the West. The satire of the spy, which concerns itself with every possible subject, is seldom acute, and never profound; while his point of view to the modern reader has become remote.

But there is, in spite of this, an interest belonging to the *Turkish Spy*—an interest which lies not only in the satire, but also in an undeveloped narrative, which introduces a love-plot, admits the reader to the intimacy of the spy's private affairs, and reveals his continual effort to avoid the police, who might at any moment turn him over to justice. An account of this Turk's passion for Doria, the beautiful Greek, recurs from time to time in the letters; and Doria's fickleness serves as a pretext for a moral lecture on the inconstancy of woman. The death of the spy's brother, the wooing, the marriage, the disappearance, and the ultimate arrival of his mother at Paris, takes the form of narration. Of chief interest, however, are the dangers which hang over the head of the Turkish spy himself, because of his secret mission to France. On one occasion the bag which contains the report to his home government is stolen, and the owner feels assured of his doom. It turns out that his servant, believing the packet to contain money, had run off with the supposed treasure, which, when he found to be mere documents that he could not read, he had buried where it was later discovered. On another occasion, for the purpose of concealing his identity, the spy involved himself in a murder. It is later disclosed that the murdered man was Doria's husband; and that Doria herself submits to the embraces of the spy in order to gain proof of his guilt. On the whole, however, the various narrative elements are not drawn together; interest in them is merely casual. The attempt at story-telling in the *Turkish Spy* is as unsuccessful as the attempt at satire. Yet great credit is due to Marana for bringing together, for the first time, the elements of which such later works as the *Lettres Persanes* and *The Citizen of the World* were composed.

Goldsmith's debt to Marana is indisputable. The *Turkish Spy* is the first and classic example of a pseudo-letter series by a foreign satirist. In France its popularity was tremendous; in England it had run through twenty-six editions before Goldsmith's death. Goldsmith knew it, and was aware of its critical method. That he was reflecting upon it at an early date is shown by his letter to his uncle Contarine, in which he compares his own position at Edinburgh to that of the Turkish spy at Paris.[3] That he was aware of the full value of Marana's scheme is best illustrated by his quotation from Voltaire in his review of the *Universal History*.[4] Voltaire here demonstrates Montesquieu's superior handling of the device, but he as clearly points out the value of the device itself: 'That satire which in the mouth of an Asiatic is poignant, would lose all force coming from an European'—and that satiric device was Marana's. So when Goldsmith wrote a book formed on exactly the same scheme as this work whose merits he quotes, and whose plan he defines, his partial debt to that author must be acknowledged, even though he may have had greater reason to imitate the more successful Montesquieu in the same manner.

In *The Citizen of the World* is found this close analogy to the *Turkish Spy*. The letters, which were mentioned in the

[3] In a letter to the Rev. Thomas Contarine, [Edinburg] May 8, 1753, Goldsmith says, 'Here as recluse as the Turkish Spy at Paris, I am almost unknown to everybody, except some few who attend the professors of physic as I do.' Quoted from *Works* I. 418.

[4] See above, p. 9.

latter as being accidentally discovered in a garret, become epistolary contributions to a daily newspaper; the philosophic Turkish spy becomes a philosophic Chinese wanderer; the foibles of Parisian life become the foibles of London life; and the satire of France becomes the satire of England.

Another point of striking analogy, which has not received mention in the past, is the common attempt at narrative interest. In the *Turkish Spy* there is, indeed, no unified story; yet there is the effort made for narrative interest. A similar appeal is found in Goldsmith's disjointed but constantly recurring story of Hingpo, the Chinese philosopher's son, and his beloved Zelis, the beautiful captive. The adventures of these two may be compared with the love-story of the Turkish spy and Doria, the beautiful Greek; and the dangers of Hingpo may be compared to the dangers of the spy. There is no similarity of detail; yet there is similarity of purpose.

There is nothing in the *Turkish Spy* of which one can definitely say that it contributed detail to *The Citizen of the World*. There is the bare possibility that a sentiment expressed by the spy may have suggested to Goldsmith something of the spirit of his Oriental wanderer:

> The whole earth is but as one country or Province, common to Men and Beasts. 'T is our Element, and therefore we ought to be free in it, to range where we please, as Fowles do in the Air, and Fish do in the Sea, without any Law, Restraint, or Injury. Such a thought as this made Socrates when he was ask'd *What Countryman he was?* answer, I am a Native of the Universe, and therefore free to live where I will.

Other parallels are found in the incidents of the maiden lady who staked her clothes, her teeth, and finally her left eye in a gamble;[5] and in the anecdote of the emperor

---

[5] Compare *Chinese Letters,* Letter CI, January 13, 1761, with the *Turkish Spy* 5. 28.

who went into the garden and killed his small daughter. In the first of these there is no close resemblance between the two accounts, while there is another version of the second story which more nearly resembles Goldsmith's.[6]

2. 1713. ADDISON, JOSEPH. *Spectator* No. 50, April 27, 1711.

Spectator No. 50,[7] written by Addison, employs a device closely akin to that of *The Citizen of the World*. The Spectator learns that four Indian kings are visiting London and watches them closely; for he is desirous of learning what ideas they have conceived of England. After their departure, a bundle of papers written by one of them is found, and the contents translated. These papers contained satirical observations by the Orientals. The satire is broad and brief, and concerns religion and politics. Brief comment also is made on the curious fashion among women of wearing patches, and on the strangeness of their manner of dressing the hair. The essay closes with a comment on the absurdity of wearing breeches and petticoats, and a promise to continue the account of the observations of the Indian kings in future *Spectator* papers. The promise was never fulfilled. The purpose of the essay is expressed in the last sentence:

> I cannot likewise forbear observing, That we are all guilty in some measure of the same narrow way of Thinking, which we meet with in this Abstract of the *Indian* Journal; when we fancy the Customs, Dresses, and Manners of other Countries are ridiculous and extravagant, if they do not resemble those of our own.[8]

The general plan of the essay, it will be noticed, is the same as the scheme of the *Chinese Letters*. And it is possible that Goldsmith specifically took from Addison's paper the hint to satirize the 'pretence of devotion' at

[6] Du Halde, *General History*. See below, p. 101.
[7] For further discussion, see p. 138, note 1.
[8] *Spectator*, No. 50, ed. 1712, I. 282.

services in St. Paul's. This topic is treated in *Chinese Letter* XL, which appeared in the *Public Ledger,* May 28, 1760.[9] It deals with the lack of reverence in the members of the congregation, who spend their time admiring one another, making love, taking snuff, and even sleeping during the sermon. The portion of Addison's essay to which Goldsmith's bears a resemblance reads:

> It is probable that when this great Work [building St. Paul's] was begun, which must have been many Hundred Years ago, there was some Religion among this People [the English]; for they give it the Name of a Temple, and have a Tradition that it was designed for Men to pay their Devotions in. And indeed, there are several Reasons which make us think, that the Natives of this Country had formerly among them some sort of Worship; for they set apart every seventh Day as sacred: But upon my going into one of these holy Houses on that Day, I could not observe any Circumstances of Devotion in their Behaviour: There was indeed a Man in Black who was mounted above the rest, and seemed to utter something with a great deal of Vehemence; but as for those underneath him, instead of paying their Worship to the Deity of the Place, they were most of them bowing and curtisying to one another, and a considerable Number of them fast asleep.

There is not enough evidence to enable us to say that Goldsmith took the suggestion of his letter from Addison; but there is a possibility, or even a probability, that he did. The *Spectator* was well known to him, as to all men of his generation; he had it in his own library.[10] His *Chinese Letters* were a continuation of the journalistic tradition made possible by Addison and Steele. Their writings

[9] *Citizen of the World,* Letter XLI.
[10] See catalogue of Goldsmith's books 'sold at auction,' which is reprinted in Prior, *Life* 2. 453-8.

certainly served him as a model for his own satiric essays. It would be hard to believe that Goldsmith was not familiar with the paper on the Indian Kings in the *Spectator*. That being the case, it is easy to imagine that he amplified the topic of irreverence at St. Paul's, which is so briefly treated by Addison, into an entire letter in the *Public Ledger*.[11]

3. 1721. MONTESQUIEU, C. DE SECONDAT, BARON DE. *Les Lettres Persanes.* Paris, 1721.[12]

With Montesquieu's *Lettres Persanes* the *genre* of pseudo-letters reached its culmination in France. All the other Oriental pseudo-letters are vastly inferior to it in satire, in wit, and in story. Goldsmith's frequent references to Montesquieu's work need not be repeated here.[13] It is sufficient to recall that he wrote of it admiringly, and that he quoted at length Voltaire's laudatory review, which stated that the *Lettres Persanes* had won for their author membership in the French Academy. There can be little doubt that the *Lettres Persanes* were a great inspiration to Goldsmith, and that he hoped to gain, through his *Chinese Letters,* at least some degree of the fame in England which his predecessor had won in France.

The *Lettres Persanes* are too well known to require much discussion here. Certain facts concerning them must be called to mind, however, in order to show *The Citizen of the World*'s similarity to them. The general scheme of the book is this: Two Persians, Usbek and his companion,

---

[11] For further possible use of the *Spectator,* see below pp. 140, 142.
[12] In studying this source, I have made careful comparison of the French original with the English translation. The first translation was made by Mr. Ozell in 1730; the third edition of his work appeared in 1731; an anonymous translation, the sixth edition, was printed in 1773.
[13] See above, p. 9.

Rica, have gone to France, because of—as Usbek expresses it—'l'envie que j'avois de m'instruire dans les sciences de l'Occident.'[14]   At Paris they proceed to satirize the customs, habits, morals, institutions, and conduct of the French, by comparing them with those of Persia.   The effectiveness of their satire is due largely to the fact that they are educated foreigners from a country supposedly less civilized than France, and to the fact that their intelligent and witty observations often reveal the superiority of Persian understanding.   The main emphasis of Montesquieu's work is on this satire, which is revealed in the letters of Usbek and Rica to their numerous correspondents at home.   The interest is diversified by the replies of their correspondents. A secondary interest is aimed at in the story of the infidelity of Usbek's favorite wife, Roxane, the death of her lover, the revolt of all his harem, and her suicide in the end.   The exciting letters from the wives and eunuchs in the seraglio form a sort of narrative frame-tale to the critical letters of the correspondents.

Montesquieu pretends to have come upon this interesting correspondence in the following way, and he offers it to the public as an anonymous translation :[15]

> Les Persanes qui écrivent ici étoient logés 'avec moi; nous passions notre vie ensemble. Comme ils me regardoient comme un homme d'un autre monde, ils ne me cachoient rien.   En effet, des gens transplantés de si loin ne pouvoient plus avoir de secrets.   Ils me communiquoient la plûpart de leurs Lettres; je les copiai. J'en surpris même quelques-unes, dont ils se seroient bien gardés de me faire confidence, tant elles étoient mortifiantes pour la vanité et la jalousie persane.
>
> Je ne fais donc que l'office de Traducteur: toute ma peine a été de mettre l'Ouvrage à nos mœurs.

[14] Montesquieu, *Œuvres,* 1764, 5. 23.
[15] *Œuvres* 5. 6.

The above statement of the circumstances of the publication of the pseudo-letters is taken from Montesquieu's preface. It need not be stated, of course, that the facts given by Montesquieu are imaginary, and that they were invented merely to afford a plausible explanation of his possessing the letters which offered such an effective vehicle of satire.

The general plan in the *Lettres Persanes* and in *The Citizen of the World* is precisely the same; in fact, in the use of the elements of the pseudo-letter, Goldsmith's work resemble Montesquieu's more closely, perhaps, than that of any other author. The close parallelism will be made clearer by the following table, which reveals the common elements of Goldsmith's and Montesquieu's pseudo-letters:

Common Elements of the Device	in *Les Lettres Persanes*	in *The Citizen of the World*
1 Oriental hero of great intelligence	A Persian	A Chinese
2 Occidental country criticized	France	England
3 Series of letters	From the Persians in Europe to friends in Persia	From the Chinese in Europe to friends in China
4 Answers to them	From Persia, giving details of family affairs, etc.	From China, giving details of family affairs, etc.
5 Description of the countries passed through on the voyage from	Persia to Paris	China to London
6 Frame-tale of love and adventure	Concerning Roxane, etc.	Concerning Hingpo, Zelis
7 Autobiographical material revealed in the persons of	Usbek	The Man-in-Black
8 Pretended translation by the anonymous editor	Montesquieu	Goldsmith

Besides the above analogy, it must be remembered that the primary purpose of each work was satiric (the satire aimed to expose the foibles of the Occident by praising the Orient), and that the secondary purpose was entertainment by story-telling, and by describing a fascinating exotic background.

This parallelism is striking; and in general scheme it is closer than any of Goldsmith's other sources. On the other hand, it is not to be expected that Goldsmith (as it will later be shown he did with D'Argens' and Lyttelton's more obscure pseudo-letters) actually pillaged much concrete material. Montesquieu's *Lettres Persanes* was too familiar a work from which to borrow with hope of concealment. Plagiarism of that sort would have been noticed immediately.

It is of course impossible that two kindred satirical works could exist without satirizing some of the same subjects. Human foibles are much the same throughout the world and in all ages; French foibles and English foibles in the eighteenth century were naturally alike, for the conditions in France and England led to similar weaknesses. Therefore one finds that Goldsmith and Montesquieu sometimes treated the same topics. That Goldsmith may have had numerous ideas suggested by Montesquieu is highly probable. What ideas he actually took from the *Lettres Persanes* cannot, of course, be ascertained with certainty. It can be said definitely, however, that the ideas found in Montesquieu did not occur in similar order in Goldsmith; and that Goldsmith made comparatively little use of detail occurring in the writing of his French predecessor.

In some cases, however, there is enough evidence for the statement that there is a strong probability that Goldsmith did avail himself of specific suggestion from Montesquieu. The first of these is found in the use of the name *Zelis,* which occurs in the *Lettres Persanes;* it was also chosen by Goldsmith for his 'beautiful captive' in love with Hingpo.

He absurdly gives this Oriental name to the niece of the Man-in-Black, Altangi's guide and companion. It seems probable that, attracted by the name in the pages of Montesquieu (where it is applied to one of the wives in the Persian seraglio of Usbek), he took it for the heroine in his own frame-tale. The fact that Hingpo met Zelis in Persia strengthens the belief that Goldsmith had it from that source. The absurdity of having the beautiful captive with a Persian name turn out in the end to be the niece of an Englishman is possibly accounted for by the fact that Goldsmith in the beginning had no idea of assuming that relationship; but, coming to the end of the series of periodical letters, the author saw that the wedding of the Chinese philosopher's son with the niece of his friend would make an effective close to the story which held together the essays. This leads one to speculate that Goldsmith had no idea, at first, how he would develop his frame-tale. Apparently, if the assumption is true, connecting the episodes of his story was not a predetermined matter, but came to the author as an afterthought. It is highly significant of, and wholly consistent with, Goldsmith's method of composing the *Chinese Letters,* as it is, indeed, with any journalistic composition.

It was not unusual for Goldsmith to take the names of his Oriental characters from some convenient source-book. As he was unfamiliar with Oriental nomenclature, this was, of course, necessary. It was true not only in the case of the name Zelis, but also in the cases of the names of Lien Chi and Fum Hoam.

Of more significance is the fact that Letter XXII of the *Lettres Persanes* suggested a scheme to Goldsmith of silencing critics who insisted that the Chinese authorship of the communications to the *Public Ledger* was fraudulent. It has been stated that the Oriental composition of Goldsmith's letters was doubted almost from the beginning, and that he, as editor, attempted to defend their authenticity. He devoted the entire *Chinese Letter,* Letter XXXI,[16] to an attempt to convince the public that a Chinese wrote the letters appearing in the *Public Ledger.* To do so he made use of a passage from Voltaire.

Careful examination of the following texts will disclose few verbal echoes, but it will show that every sentence in one has its counterpart in the other, in the same sequence; the idea in both, it should be observed, is developed by means of a military metaphor:

MONTESQUIEU.

Je n'ai jamais vu un décisionnaire si universel: son esprit ne fut jamais suspendu par le moindre doute. On laissa les sciences; on parla des nouvelles du tems: il décida sur les nouvelles du tems. Je voulus l'attraper, et je dis en moi-même: 'Il faut que je me mette dans mon fort; je vais me refugier dans mon pays.' Je lui parlai de la Perse. Mais, à peine lui eus-je dit quatre mots qu'il me donna deux démentis, fondé sur l'autorité de MM. Tavernier et Chardin. 'Ah! bon Dieu! dis-je en moi-même, quel homme est-ce là? Il connoîtra tout à l'heure les rues d'Ispahan mieux que moi!' Mon parti fut bientôt pris: je me tus, je le laissai parler, et il décide encore.'[17]

GOLDSMITH.

The moment I ventured to speak, I was at once contradicted with a snap. I attempted, by a second and a third assault, to retrieve my lost reputation, but was still beat back with confusion. I was resolved to

---

[16] *Public Ledger,* April 25, 1760; *The Citizen of the World,* Letter XXXII.

[17] *Lettres Persanes,* Letter LXXII, ed. Barckhausen, 1913, p. 145.

attack him once more from entrenchment, and turned the conversation upon the government of China: but even here he asserted, snapped, and contradicted as before. 'Heavens,' thought I, 'this man pretends to know China even better than myself.' I looked round to see who was on my side; but every eye was fixed in admiration on the great man: I therefore at last thought proper to sit silent, and act the pretty gentleman during the ensuing conversation.[18]

The resemblance of these passages is apparent to the reader only upon careful examination; and yet study of them affords conviction of the fact that the conversation between Altangi and the one who rudely contradicts him is drawn from the passage satirizing the 'universal dogmatist.' It is necessary to have the texts in juxtaposition in order to detect similarity. In using a source so well known as the *Lettres Persanes,* Goldsmith took pains to avoid detection; and it is almost certain that the resemblance would escape a casual reader. Of the passages rewritten from sources, this is the only one which I have found that Goldsmith has not improved.

A third analogy between one of the *Chinese Letters* and a portion of the *Lettres Persanes* is seen in the moralistic political satire called 'The rise and decline of the kingdom of Lao,' which bears a resemblance to the *Histoire des Troglodites.* This history, first told by Montesquieu, is avowedly imitated and continued in Lyttelton's *Persian Letters.* Goldsmith's *Chinese Letter* XI[19] is an apparent imitation of one or both of these accounts. There is more evidence for the belief that Lyttelton's letter was Goldsmith's source; so the discussion of it is placed, to avoid repetition, under that portion of this work which concerns Lyttelton's *Persian Letters.*[20]

[18] *Works* 3. 280; *The Citizen of the World,* Letter LXXII.
[19] April 1, 1760; *The Citizen of the World,* Letter XXV.
[20] See below, pp. 52-8.

Many other similarities exist in the writings of these two satirists; but they are of such a nature that the evidence of borrowing is not conclusive.[21]

4. 1735. LYTTELTON, GEORGE, FIRST BARON (1709-1733). *Letters from a Persian in England to his friend at Ispahan.* London, 1735.

George Lyttelton's *Persian Letters* is the first collection of pseudo-letters in imitation of Montesquieu and Marana which was originally written in English. The author in his notice 'To the Bookseller' says:[22]

> I Need not acquaint you by what Accident these Letters were put into my Hands, and what Pains I have taken in translating them.... I have acquired Skill enough in the *Persian* Tongue, to be able to give the Sense of them pretty justly: Though I must acknowledge my Translation far inferior to the *Eastern Sublimity* of the Original....
> But whoever reads them with Attention, will be convinced, that they are certainly the work of a perfect Stranger.

A perusal of the work will convince the reader of quite the contrary, and confirm the opinion gained from various authorities on Lyttelton's life ... that it is a pseudo-translation written in English by Lyttelton.[23]

Lyttelton states that his *Persian Letters* are a continua-

---

[21] For an example of this sort, compare *The Citizen of the World*, Letter XXI (*Works* 3. 78) with *Lettres Persanes*, Letter XXVIII (ed. Barckhausen, 1913, pp. 55-6). In these passages, both writers compare the occupants of boxes at the theatre to actors in a dumb show, and immediately follow this with a description of ogling and love-making.

[22] Lyttelton, *Persian Letters*, fifth edition, London, 1744, pp. 3-5.

[23] Conant, *The Oriental Tale in England*, p. 179.

tion of the original French *Lettres Persanes*. In Chapter I
he say that the 'Relations' received from Usbek 'of those
Parts of *Europe* which he had seen' inspired a continuation
of the account from England.[24] Again in Letter X the
author acknowledges his imitation of Montesquieu, giving an
avowed continuation of the 'History of the Troglodites'
begun in the *Lettres Persanes*.[25] The imitation, however, is
vastly inferior to the original.

The inferiority is due partly to the fact that all of the
epistles are written by Selim at London to his friend Mirza
at Ispahan. This one-sided correspondence lacks the
variety which is one of the chief charms of the letters in
the earlier *Lettres Persanes,* and in the later *The Citizen
of the World.*

But in another respect Lyttelton is more successful.
When, like the authors of both the above works, he aims at
narrative interest by interspersing his letters with stories,
he holds the reader's attention. Letter XXXI makes an
attempt at this interest. It is a long tale of the marriage of
Polydore and Emilia, who consummated their wedding
vows only after twenty years of trials and separation.[26]
This letter is in reality a fifty-page digression from the
account of Usbek's actions in England, and is introduced
simply for the sake of diverting the reader with a narrative.
Another story of this character is that of Ludovica and
Honoria.[27]

While these tales are both digressions from the account
of the adventures of Lyttleton's Persian satirist, there is
another story in the *Persian Letters* which, by reason of
Selim's participation in it, forms a frame-tale to the entire
series of letters. It begins in Letter XXII with the intro-

---

[24] Lyttelton, *Persian Letters,* pp. 7-8.
[25] See above p. 55.
[26] Lyttelton, *Persian Letters,* pp. 103-150.
[27] *Ibid.,* pp. 24-33.

duction of the first character, Abdallah. In Letter XLII the actual narrative begins; it tells of Abdallah's going to Malta for the purpose of ransoming his father, and describes his sadness at being separated from his wife, Zelis. Letter LXXVIII concludes the tale with a long account of the hero's adventures on his travels.

It is highly probable that from this story in the *Persian Letters* Goldsmith received suggestion for the frame-tale in the *Chinese Letters*. Similarity is found in the following episodes which are common to both: the use of the name Zelis for the heroines,[28] the attack by a pirate ship, the ransom of the captive, the separation of father and son, the attempt to make one of the characters renounce his religion in favor of another, the capture of the heroine, the sudden appearance of the beautiful slave to the hero, her attempted flight with the hero, and the separation and final reunion of hero and the heroine. While the working out of Lyttleton's plot differs greatly from the story of Zelis and Hingpo, the occurrence of so many common elements makes it reasonable to believe that Goldsmith drew at least some suggestions from the clumsy frame-table of Lyttelton's *Persian Letters*.

That he had further inspiration from either Lyttelton or Montesquieu is more than likely. The reader may judge from the following: Montesquieu relates in his *Lettres Persanes* XI-XIV the history of the Troglodytes, a small race of people who resided in Arabia.[29] This narrative teaches the moral that as long as a nation lives in a state of nature, occupying itself with domestic relations, and neglecting the complicated problems of government, it will endure in happiness and opulence. Montesquieu's story deals with the various religious and social pleasures which

[28] For a discussion of the use of the name *Zelis,* see also above, pp. 48-9.

[29] Pp. 45-52.

were the birthright of the Troglodites as long as they lived in their native simplicity; and it suggests that they would relapse to their former barbarity if they abandoned simple interests. At this point Montesquieu leaves the story.

Lyttelton, in his *Persian Letters* X-XXI,[30] continues the 'History of the Troglodites,' acknowledging that it is a continuation of Usbek's narrative. According to Lyttelton, the Troglodites soon reached such a condition of opulence that they attracted an invasion by a neighboring race. They defeated the enemy at home, and then carried the battle into their neighbors' territory. Here they were again victorious. The conquered lands were divided, and now with interests no longer centred at home, and with too much opulence, the Troglodites developed luxurious habits, became arrogant, abandoned their 'state of nature' for a condition of complex government, and thus became utterly without moral scruple. Their standard of happiness was now no longer liberty, but riches.

Goldsmith's *Chinese Letter* XXI is a moral, political satire which is probably based on the 'History of the Troglodites.' The story which Goldsmith (in *The Citizen of the World* edition) gives the heading, 'The Rise and Decline of the Kingdom of Lao,' concerns a small country north of China. The inhabitants of this land lived in primitive simplicity, and were interested only in domestic affairs. The virtue of the citizens brought prosperity to the land, and prosperity led to opulence. The people then began to long for a more complicated system of government. At this time, invited by the riches of Lao, the Tartars invaded the kingdom. They were repulsed. The defenders pursued them into their own country, conquered it, and divided the land among the inhabitants of Lao. This expansion of Lao was the ruin of its people; for the increased opulence thus given them

[30] Pp. 43-78.

led to luxury, voluptuousness, and degradation. Domestic affairs of the nation were neglected; wealth was considered the only sign of happiness. The excesses of the people impoverished and weakened them, so that they soon became the prey of an invading army, and the kingdom of Lao was subjected to the rule of China.

Goldsmith tells this history in order to argue against a British foreign policy of expansion. He hoped by telling it to illustrate the dangers to home interest of a too ambitious desire for colonies. Editors and biographers have given Goldsmith much credit for understanding the political situation of the time.[31] It is true that his essay shows much insight; but the idea was certainly not original with him. It was suggested by Montesquieu in his history of the Troglodites to Lyttelton, who expanded it, and by Lyttelton to Goldsmith, who in his turn expanded it from applying to mere complexity of government to a condemnation of a too broad commercial policy. Goldsmith probably read both Lyttelton's and Montesquieu's versions of the story, and was influenced by both; but in writing Letter XXI he apparently followed more of the details of the former writer's continuation.

In *Chinese Letter,* Letter XIII, is found another example of Goldsmith's use of sources.[32] The substance of this essay is taken directly from Letter LXVIII of Lyttelton's *Persian Letters.* The texts of both Lyttelton and Goldsmith are given below:

Selim *to* Mirza *at* Ispahan. From *London.*	*From Lien Chi Altangi to Fum Hoam.*
The other Morning, a Friend of mine came to me, and told me, with the Air of one who	I WAS some days ago agreeably surprised by a message from a lady of distinction, who sent

---

[31] See Moore, *Life of Oliver Goldsmith,* Index.
[32] *Public Ledger,* February 28, 1760.

brings an agreeable Piece of News, that there was a Lady who most passionately desired the Pleasure of my Acquaintance, and had commissioned him to carry me to see her.—I will not deny to thee, that my Vanity was a little flattered with this Message: I fancied she had seen me in some public Place, and taken a liking to my Person; not being able to comprehend what other Motive could make her send for a Man she was a Stranger to in so free and extraordinary a Manner. I painted her in my own imagination very young, and very handsome, and set out with most pleasing Expectations, to see the Conquest I had made:

But when I arrived at the Place of Assignation, I found a little old Woman very dirty, encircled by four or five strange Fellows, one of whom had a Paper in his Hand, which he was reading to her with all the Emphasis of an Author.[33]

me word. that she most passionately desired the Pleasure of my acquaintance; and, with the utmost impatience, expected an interview. I will not deny my dear Fum Hoam, but that my vanity was raised at such an invitation, I flattered myself that she had seen me in some public place, and had conceived an affection for my person, which thus induced her to deviate from the usual decorums of the sex.

My imagination painted her in all the bloom of youth and beauty. I fancied her tended by the loves and graces, and I set out with the most pleasing expectations of seeing the conquest I had made.

When I was introduced into her apartment, my expectations were quickly at an end; I perceived a little shrivelled figure indolently reclined on a sofa, who nodded by way of approbation at my approach.[34]

The remainder of Goldsmith's essay satirizes the absurd pretense of English faddists to understand Chinese manners. In Lyttelton's essay there is similar pretense by the lady of distinction of a knowledge of Oriental religion. In this instance, Goldsmith has taken the situation, closely copied

---

[33] *Persian Letters*, pp. 277-8.

[34] Quoted from *Public Ledger* text. *The Citizen of the World* text is unchanged. See *The Citizen of the World*, Letter XIV.

the phraseology, and built up his essay with details of his own selection.[35]

It was not unusual for Goldsmith in this way to make use of books, not only to get suggestions for satirical topics, but also for the actual pillaging of concrete material, which he at times incorporated word for word into his own text.[36]

5. BOYER (JEAN BAPTISTE DE) (MARQUIS D'ARGENS), *Lettres Chinoises, ou Correspondance Philosophique, Historique et Critique, Entre un Chinois Voyageur et ses Correspondans à la Chine, en Moscovie, en Perse, et au Japon. Nouvelle Edition, Augmentée de nouvelles Lettres et de quantité de Remarques....* A La Haye, 1755.[37]

The *Lettres Chinoises* of the Marquis D'Argens not only served as a general model for *The Citizen of the World*, but also contributed specific material for several of its essays.[38] As they are described on the title-page, the letters are philosophical, historical, and critical. They comprise a series from Sioeu-Tcheou at Paris to Yn-Che-Chan at Pekin, in China. So this work of D'Argens is directly parallel in device to the later work of Goldsmith, which, while appearing in the *Public Ledger,* was known by the same title, the

[35] See Conant, *The Oriental Tale in England,* pp. 183 ff., for discussion of this parallelism.

[36] The facts only are given in this section. A discussion of the sources with relation to its effect on Goldsmith's method of composition will be found on pp. 114-24.

[37] First printed in 1739 (Lanson, *Manuel Bibliographique de la Literature Française Moderne* (Paris, 1909-12), Nos. 9894, 10,199), Fifth edition, 1776. All references in this work are to the edition of 1775. An English translation, under the title, *Chinese Letters,* appeared in 1741, and was reprinted as *The Chinese Spy* in 1751.

[38] That Goldsmith used the French original, and not the English translations, is easily shown by a comparison of the texts.

Chinese Letters. Prior notes[39] that the relinquishment of this title (in favor of *The Citizen of the World*) 'arose probably from a production of the Marquis D'Argens' translated into English in 1741, being extant under the same title.' So Goldsmith's pseudo-letters and D'Argens' pseudo-letters were not only identical in plan, but also, for a period of two years, were popularly known by the same name.

Goldsmith, whose meagre knowledge of the Orient made the writing of Eastern letters a difficult problem, found D'Argens' kindred work of great assistance, especially at first, when he was seeking a convincingly exotic background. So in a great many instances he availed himself of details, and even philosophic conclusions, set forth in the *Lettres Chinoises.* The insulting glances to which his philosopher was subjected while walking the city streets, the different standards of Oriental and Occidental beauty, the dissimilar features of Chinese and European women, with the conclusion drawn that 'What is a Deformity in China is counted a Beauty in Europe,' the Oriental fear of death, and many other details, are found in the pages of the Marquis D'Argens.

While Goldsmith's first few letters contain numerous incidents which are identical with D'Argens' incidents, Letter VIII[40] in the *Public Ledger,* which appeared on February 12, 1760, finds its source as a whole in the *Lettres Chinoises.* Goldsmith's paper satirizes English law and religion, the rigidity of which as applied to marriage rites, causes, particularly among men of fashion, the prevalence of immorality and prostitution. D'Argens' essay deals with the same topic. The closeness with which Goldsmith followed the text of his source is apparent from the parallel columns printed below:

[39] *Life* 1. 397.
[40] *The Citizen of the World,* Letter IX.

D'ARGENS, LETTRE XXI.

GOLDSMITH, LETTER VIII.

Les François ne peuvent avoir, ainsi que tu le sais, cher Yn-Che-Chan, qu'une seule femme légitime; leur Religion leur défend l'usage des concubines; les Loix civiles le leur interdisent aussi. On croiroit d'abord qu'il n'y a aucun pays dans l'Univers, où les droits de l'amour & de l'hymen soient aussi resserrés & aussi restreints que dans celui-ci; il n'en est point cependant, où ils en aient de plus étendus. Les Chinois ont moins de liberté, moins de privilége, & moins de commodités, malgré les concubines, ou secondes femmes qu'ils peuvent avoir par l'autorité des Loix.

Their laws and religion forbid the English to keep more than one woman, I therefore concluded that prostitutes were banished from society; I was deceived, every man here keeps as many wives as he can maintain, the laws are praised and disregarded.

Les François, je te l'ai dit, cher Yn-Che-Chan, ont plusieurs regles, ordonnées par les Juges Civils & Ecclésiastiques, qui ne sont jamais mises en exécution: elles sont faites uniquement pour orner leurs Livres de Droit. On peut les regarder comme les anciens Ouvrages des Sibylles, que gardoient dans leur Temples les Prêtres Romains: on les respectoit beaucoup, quoiqu'on ne les lût jamais & qu'on ne les entendit pas même. La Loi, donc, qui leur ordonne de n'avoir qu'une seule femme légitime, n'est observée que par ceux, qui faute de bien, n'ont pas le pouvoir de la violer, ou par quelques personnes à qui une seule femme suffit; le reste des François n'y a aucun égard & la viole publiquement. On entend dire tous les jours; un tel Duc

The very Chinese,

whose religion allows him two wives, takes not half the liberties of an Englishman in this particular.

The English laws

may be compared to the books of the Sibyls,

they are held in great veneration, but seldom read, or seldomer understood. . . . The law therefore which commands them to have but one wife, is strictly observed only by those for whom one is more than sufficient, or by such as have not money to buy two. As for the rest

they violate it publicly. . . . A mandarine therefore here generally keeps four wives, a gentleman three, and a stage-player

entretient deux filles fort jolies, il a outre cela une Danseuse de l'Opera; un tel Magistrat donne deux mille écus par an à une jeune Languedocienne, qu'il a logée auprès de chez lui; cette petite couturiere a un marchand sur son compte. Enfin dans tous les Etats l'usage d'avoir des concubines est également établi. . . . l'adultere: ce vice passe à Paris & dans tout le Royaume parmi les gens du monde pour une galanterie. On appelle ici un adultere, un *homme à bonne fortune;* on donne le titre d' *aimable* à une personne qui mérite celui d' *abominable.*[41]

two. As for the magistrates, the county justices and squires, are employed in debauching young virgins for the town; and the city justices are employed in sending them to the house of correction. Thus they play into each others hands, and make work for each other. . . .

There are also another set of men, [men of fashion] whose whole employment consists in corrupting beauty wherever they are admitted; these the silly part of the sex call amiable; the more sensible part of them, and all the men however give them the title of abominable.[42]

Again on Feb. 14, 1760, in *Chinese Letters,* Letter IX, we find Goldsmith following, in his essay to the *Public Ledger,* the text of one of D'Argens' *Lettres Chinoise.* This time the topic was the funeral rites of the Daures, to which is prefaced a description of the country surrounding the Great Wall of China. Goldsmith's narrative very closely follows the text of D'Argens' *Lettres Chinoises,* Letter XXVIII. It will be noted that, in using his source, Goldsmith did two things: he condensed the material by nearly one-half, and he made great changes in style. Parallel columns of both D'Argens' and Goldsmith's texts follow:

D'ARGENS, LETTRE XXVIII.
Tiac, à Sioeu-Tcheou.

JE suis arrivé depuis deux jours à Moscou. Je ne saurois dire, mon cher Sioeu-Tcheou, combien j'ai essuyé de fatigues

GOLDSMITH, LETTER IX.
From Lien Chi Altangi, to Fum Hoam. . . .

I Have hitherto given you no account of my journey from China to Europe. . . .

[41] D'Argens, *Lettres Chinoises,* Letter XXI, ed. 1775, I. 208-210.
[42] Goldsmith, *Chinese Letters,* Letter VIII; *The Citizen of the World,* Letter IX.

dans mon voyage. Tu dois comprendre aisement les embarras & les peines qu'on essuye en traversant tant de pays differens, la plûpart déserts, ou habités par des Barbares; car c'est ainsi qu'on doit appeller tous les peuples qui séparent l'Empire de la Chine & de la Moscovie. Quoiqu'ils soient presque tous soumis à l'un ou à l'autre de ces deux Empires, ils ressemblent cependant très-peu aux Nations dont ils relevent. Tu seras sans doute bien aise d'être instruit des mœurs & des coutumes de ces peuples, presque inconnus au reste de l'Univers. Je contenterai ta curiosité le mieux qu'il me sera possible. . . .

Après avoir passé la grande muraille, je trouvai quelques villes entierement dépeuplées; elles paroissoient, par leurs ruines, avoir été très-considerables. On y voit des Temples fort beaux, des statues qui viennent d'une bonne main: tout cela est entierment abandonné. Je demandois à mes guides quelle avoit été la cause du dévastement

total de ce pays. L'un d'eux, qui paroissoit savoir l'histoire, me dit qu'il y avoit plusieurs siécles qu'un Prince Tartare qui faisoit sa résidence dans la principale de ces villes ruinées, eut la guerre avec un de nos Empereurs, qui l'ayant vaincu,

You will easily conceive The fatigue of crossing vast tracts of land,

either desolate, or still more dangerous in its inhabitants. The retreats of men, who seem driven from society, in order to make war upon all the human race; for tho' they nominally profess a subjection either to Moscovy or China, they have no resemblance of the countries on which they depend.

After I had crossed the great wall, the first object that presented were the remains of desolated cities, and all the magnifice of venerable ruin. There were to be seen temples of beautiful structure, statues wrought by the hand of a master, and around a country of luxuriant plenty; but not one single inhabitant to reap the bounties of nature. These were prospects that might humble the pride of kings, and repress human vanity. I ask'd my guide the cause of such desolation.

These countries, says he, were once the dominions of a Tartar prince; and these ruins once the seat of opulence, arts, and ease. This prince waged an unsuccessful war with one of the emperors of China; he was conquered, his cities plundered, and all his

le chassa de ses Etats, & en fit esclaves tous les habitans. C'est ainsi qu'on voit quelquefois, cher Sioeu-Tcheou, tout un peuple périr par la faute de son Souverain, ou par la cruauté d'un autre.

Je marchai encore quelques jours avant d'arriver chez les Daures. Xaixigar est la principale de leurs villes; elle est cependant assez petite. Les autres, qui sont au nombre de cinq ou six, ne peuvent être regardées que comme des villages. Ces peuples sont sujets de notre Empereur, & se soumettent avec respect à tous les ordres qu'il lui plait de leur prescrire. Les Gouverneurs & les autres Officiers qui sont envoyés de la Cour pour exiger le tribut, abusant de leur autorité, prennent souvent les femmes à leurs maris, & s'en servent, comme si cela leur appartenoit de droit. Les Daures, accoutumés à une obeissance aveugle, ne murmurent point, ou du moins ne murmurent qu'en secret contre une pareille violence. La nécessité & la coutume leur ont appris à pratiquer ce que l'ambition & la politique font faire à tant de courtisans François, qui mettent à profit la tendresse du Prince, ou de ses Ministres, & souffrent patiem-

subjects carried into captivity. Such are the effects of the ambition of kings![43] sure, my friend, the cruelty and the pride of man have made more desarts than nature ever made! she is kind, but man is ungrateful! Proceeding in my journey thro' this pensive scene of desolated beauty, in a few days I arrived among the Daures. . . .

Xaixigar is their principal city, which, compared with those of Europe, scarcely deserves the name.

. . . . a nation still dependent on China. . . .[44]

The governors and other officers, who are sent yearly from Pekin, abuse their authority, and often take the wives and daughters of the inhabitants to themselves.

The Daures accustomed to base submission, feel no resentment at those injuries, or stifle what they feel.

Custom and necessity teach even barbarians the same arts of dissimulation that ambition and intrigue inspire in the breasts of courtiers.[45] Upon beholding such unlicensed stretches of power, alas, thought I, how little does our wise and good emperor

---

[43] The first and third editions insert here: 'Ten Dervises, says the Indian proverb, shall sleep in peace upon a single carpet, while two kings shall quarrel though they have kingdoms to divide them.'

[44] In Goldsmith's order these lines follow 'Daures,' five lines above.

[45] In *The Citizen of the World*, first and third editions, for 'courtiers' read 'the polite.'

ment les infidelités volontaires de leurs femmes.

know of these intolerable exactions! these provinces are too distant for complaint, and too insignificant to expect redress.

The more distant the government, the honester should be the governor to whom it is entrusted; for certainty of not being punished,[46] *is a strong inducement to violation.*

La Religion des Daures est plus ridicule & plus folle que celles des Sectateurs de *Lao-Kium.* Que dirois-tu, cher Sioeu-Tcheou, toi sage disciple & sectateur de *Confucius,* qui admets, ainsi que ton maître, l'existence d'un principe éternel, intelligent, auteur de tous les êtres, si tu voyois les cérémonies barbares & insensées des Daures? Combien ne déplorerois-tu pas l'aveuglement & la foiblesse de l'esprit humain? Cette raison si vantée, & qui seule est le partage des hommes, à quoi sert-elle à plusieurs? Elle leur est bien plus inutile que l'instinct accordé aux bêtes; elles agissent du moins uniformément, elles se conduisent conformément à la nature, & ne font point des choses directement opposées à ce qu'elles devroient faire. Elles trouvent dans leur instinct un guide bien plus sûr que les foibles mortels dans leur raison.

Les Daures n' adorent point un Dieu bienfaisant; ils rendent un culte superstitieux à une

The religion of the Daures is more absurd than even that of the sectaries of Fohi.

How would you be surprised, O sage disciple and follower of Confucius! you who believe

one eternal intelligent cause of all, should you be present at the barbarous ceremonies of this infatuated people. How would you deplore the blindness and folly of mankind. His boasted reason seems only to light him astray,

and brutal instinct more

regularly points out the path to happiness.

Could you think it? they adore a wicked divinity; they fear him and they worship

[46] In *The Citizen of the World,* first and third editions, for "certainty of not being punished," read "hope of impunity."

Divinité mechante, & qui se plait à persécuter les hommes. Les Chrétiens disent que cette Divinité est le diable, esprit malin qu'ils craignent presque autant que les Daures, mais qu'ils n'honorent point. Quoiqu'il en soit, voici comment ces peuples honorent cette Divinité maligne & pernicieuse. Les hommes & les femmes s'assemblent vers le milieu de la nuit dans une chambre qui leur sert de Temple. Un des assistans so couche à terre: pendant qu'il est dans cette attitude, les autres font des cris & des hurlemens affreux, ils mêlent à cette musique infernal le son d'un tambour. Après que ce bruit a duré environ deux heures, celui qui étoit couché se releve, & prenant l'air & les manieres d'un homme inspiré, il prophetise à ceux qui l' interrogent ce qui doit leur arriver.

Dans la plûpart des pays, cher Sioeu-Tcheou, ce sont les Bonses, les Bracmanes & les Prêtres, qui, abusant de la credulité des peuples, les entrainent dans les superstitions les plus grossieres; voici une Nation entiere, qui est elle-même l'auteur de ses folies: triste preuve du penchant que tous les hommes ont au fanatisme! Lorsqu'ils ne sont point trompés, ils se trompent eux-mêmes, & chez eux la superstition ne perd jamais ses droits.

Les Daures habitent dans des maisons faites de terre & couvertes de roseaux; une seule salle compose tout le bâtiment: on

him; they imagine him a malicious being, ready to injure and ready to be appeased.

The men and women assemble at midnight in a hut, which serves for a temple. A priest stretches himself on the ground, and all the people
pour forth the most horrid cries, while drums and timbrels swell the infernal concert.
After this dissonance . . . has continued about two hours, the priest rises from the ground, assumes an air of
inspiration, grows big with the inspiring demon, and pretends to a skill in futurity.

In every country, my friend, the bonzes, the brachmans, and the priests deceive the people; all reformations begin from the laity; the priests point us out the way to heaven with their fingers, but stand still themselves, nor seem to journey to the country in view.

fait un trou au milieu du plan-
cher pour laisser passer la
fumée; il y a cependant plusieurs
fenêtres qui sont placées dans
tous les côtés de la maison.

Les coutumes & les usages des
Daures répondent à leur Religion
& en sont véritablement dignes.
Ils conservent pendant trois jours
les morts; ils les placent ensuite
dans des fosses peu profondes,
où ils laissent une ouverture du
côté de la tête du cadavre.
C'est par ce trou que les parens
lui donnent tous les jours à
boire & à manger; ils lue présent-
ent les alimens à la bouche dans
une grande cuillier. Cette céré-
monie dure plusieurs jours; ensuite on couvre tout-à-fait la
fosse, & le mort n'est plus prié
de prendre quelques nourritures.
Que les hommes, cher Sioeu-
Tcheou, aient pû se persuader
qu'une chose dont ils voyoient la
destruction, qu'un cadavre qui
se pourrissoit à leurs yeux,
avoit besoin de nourriture; qu'ils
aient pù journellement lui pré-
senter des viandes, de quelle folie
ne doit-on point après cela les
croire capables?

Je le repete encore, qu'est-ce que
devient la raison chez bien des
hommes? Que dis-je chez bien
des hommes? chez des Nations
entieres, qui n'en font aucun
usage? Les Daures extravag-
uent pendant toute leur vie; ils
la passent à hurler pour invoquer
une Divinité maligne & cruelle,
à porter des viandes cuites à des
cadavres: ce sont-la leurs plus

The customs of this people
correspond to their religion;

they keep their dead for three
days on the same bed where the
person died; after which they
bury him in a grave moderately
deep, but with the head still un-
covered.

Here for several days they
present him different sorts of
meats; which, when they per-
ceive he does not consume, they
fill up the grave, and desist from
desiring him to eat for the
future.
How, how can mankind be guilty
of such strange absurdity; to
entreat a dead body already
putrid to partake of the banquet?

Where, I again repeat it, is
human reason!
     not only some men,
but whole nations, seem divested
of its illumination. Here we
observe a whole country

adoring a divinity through fear,
and attempting to feed the dead.
These are their

serieuses & leurs plus religieuses occupations. Ont-ils la raison en partage? D'où vient donc n'en font-ils aucun usage; & s'ils en font usage, quelle est cette raison qui autorise les folies les plus grandes? . . . .

Je suis persuadé, cher Sioeu-Tcheou, que, sans les Philosophes, c'est-à-dire sans ce petit nombre d'hommes vertueux qui semble être d'une autre nature que celle des autres mortels, sans ces Philosophes, dis-je, le culte d'une Divinité méchante seroit établi par toute la terre. La crainte conduit bien plus le genre humain que la reconnoissance. Pour un homme qui est vertueux, uniquement pour l'amour de la vertu, & par la reconnoissance qu'il a des biens qu'il a reçus du Ciel, il y en a dix mille qui n'évitent le crime que par l'appréhension d'en être punis. S'il y avoit un peuple persuadé, ainsi que l'étoient les Epicuriens, que les Cieux ne peuvent rien sur le malheur des hommes; ces mêmes Cieux ne seroient pas plus honorés chez lui, que la véritable Divinité l'est chez les Daures & chez les Targasins.[47]

most serious and most religious occupations: are these men rational, or are not the apes of Borneo more wise?

Certain I am, O thou instructor of my youth; that without philosophers, without some few virtuous men, who seem to be of a different nature from the rest of mankind,
without such as these the worship of a wicked Divinity would surely be established over every part of the earth. Fear guides more to their duty than gratitude: for one man who is virtuous from the love of virtue: from the obligation which he thinks he lies under to the giver of all; there are ten thousand who are good only from their apprehensions of punishment. Could these at least be persuaded,
as the Epicureans were, that heaven had no thunders in store for the villain, they would no longer continue to acknowledge subordination, or thank that being who gave them theirs. Adieu.[48]

D'Argens' Letter XXXI of the *Lettres Chinoises* is the source of Goldsmith's *Letter* XV.[49] In this case Goldsmith did not accept the structure of D'Argens' essay. He

---

[47] D'Argens, *Lettres Chinoises* I. 293-301.

[48] Goldsmith, *Chinese Letters*, No. IX; *The Citizen of the World,* Letter X.

[49] *Public Ledger*, March 11, 1760; *The Citizen of the World,* Letter XVI.

changed the order of composition materially; he omitted; he put the material together into a well ordered whole; he made more acute conclusions. In the columns of text which follow, the order of the source has been preserved. The remarks of Goldsmith have been placed opposite their parallels in D'Argens, but the order of Goldsmith's writing has been indicated, so that the reader may understand the reasons for the new structure. In spite of the length of the texts, both of them are quoted entire, as it is deemed highly necessary for drawing conclusions with regard to Goldsmith's method of composition.[50]

D'ARGENS LETTRE XXXI.
Sioeu Tcheou, à Yn-Che-Chan.

Une de mes principales occu-pations depuis que je suis à Paris, cher Yn-Che-Chan, c'est de remarquer avec soin toutes les fables & les mensonges grossiers, dont les trois quarts des Auteurs Européens remplissent leurs Ouvrages. Il semble que dans tous les tems les habitans de ces pays aient été portés à débiter les contes les plus absurdes, & qui pis est, à les débiter d'un ton grave & d'une maniere aussi affirmative que s'ils avoient dit les vérités les plus évidentes. Les Docteurs qu'on regarde en Europe avec le plus de respect, n'ont point été exempts de défaut, & ont menti aussi impu-demment que les autres; ils ont

GOLDSMITH LETTER XV.
From Lien Chi Altangi, to Fum Hoam. . . .

I Know not whether I am more obliged to the Chinese mis-sionaries for the instruction I have received from them, or by the falsehoods they have taught me to believe. . . .[51]

---

[50] In this section only the texts and facts pertaining to Goldsmith's use of sources are given. A discussion of their significance follows on pp. 114-24.

[51] Cf. Col. 1, ll. 25-34.

eu même l'effronterie de dire qu'ils avoient été les témoins des choses fabuleuses qu'ils racontoient.

Les Missionnaires nous reprochent quelquefois que nos livres sont pleins de fausses histoires & de rélations peu exactes : comment osent-ils nous faire ces reproches, eux qui devroient rougir de honte des impertinences qui sont inserées dans les trois quarts des Ouvrages de leurs compatriotes?

Pour te donner une idée, cher Yn-Che-Chan, de la hardiesse avec laquelle les Européens mentent, je te communiquerai actuellement quelques-uns des contes que j' ai lûs dans leurs anciens Auteurs & dans quelques modernes ; tu verras ainsi que ce n'est pas d'aujour'd'hui que le mensonge est en droit de tenir la place de la vérité chez les Ecrivains Européens les plus célébres.

Les bornes étroites de nos Lettres ne me permettant pas de t' apprendre toutes les choses qui m'ont frappé, je me fixerai a un seul point ; c'est à ce que les Ecrivains ont dit de la figure de certains peuples. Tu croirois que respectant du moins la vraisemblance, ils se seroient contentés de faire de leurs mœurs & de leurs coutumes les rélations les plus absurdes & les

The Europeans reproach us with false history and fabulous chronology; how ought they to blush to see their own books, many of which are written by the doctors[52] of their religion filled with the most monstrous fables, and attested with the utmost solemnity.[53]

The bounds of a letter, do not permit me to tell all the absurdities of this kind, which in my reading I have met with. I shall confine myself to the accounts which some of their lettered men give of the persons of a certain people on our globe. Not satisfied with the most solemn asseverations, they sometimes pretend to have been eye witnesses of what they describe.

[52] Cf. Col. 1, ll. 16-24.
[53] Cf. Col. 1, ll. 1-16.

plus fausses; point du tout, ils ont encore voulu leur donner une forme bizarre, entierement differente de leur nature humaine. Peu contens de s'ériger en Législateurs & d'établir des loix & des usages, ils ont voulu être créateurs; ils ont fait de nouveaux hommes, aussi differens entre-eux pour la figure, que les Chinois & les Caraïtes le sont par les mœurs & les inclinations.

Un ancien Docteur Chrétien, dans un de ses principaux Ouvrages, avoit dit qu'il n'étoit pas impossible de trouver une Nation entiere qui n'eût qu'un seul œil au milieu du front. Il ne s'en tint pas à ce premier doute; bientôt il assûre dans un autre Ouvrage que la chose étoit réelle, & qui plus est, il protesta d'en avoir été le témoin. *J'étois déja*, dit-il, *Evêque d'Hippone; lorsque je fis un voyage en Ethiopie en la compagnie de certains Serviteurs de Christ, pour y prêcher le saint Evangile, & je vis dans les Provinces Meridionales de ce pays un peuple qui n'avoit qu'on seul œil au milieu du front.*

Tu séras peut-être étonné, cher Yn-Che-Chan, de la hardiesse avec laquelle cet Auteur crée par sa seule fantaisie un peuple de Cyclopes, qui n' exista jamais que dans l'imagination des Poëtes. Il n'est pas le seul qui ait assuré une pareille fable, il l'avoit puisée dans plusieurs Ecrivains qui l'avoient précédé. Aulu-Gelle dit qu'il a trouvé

A christian doctor in one of his principal performances says that it was not impossible for a whole nation to have but one eye in the middle of the forehead. He is not satisfied with leaving it in doubt; but in another work assures us, that the fact was certain, and that he himself was an eye witness of it. *When, says he, I took a journey into Ethiopia in company with several other servants of Christ, in order to preach the gospel there; I beheld in the southern provinces of that country a nation which had only one eye in the midst of their foreheads.*

You will, no doubt, be surprized, reverend Fum Hoam, with this author's effrontery;

but alas he is not alone in this story; he has only borrowed it from several others who wrote before him.

dans des Auteurs anciens qu'il y a une certaine Nation parmi les Scythes qui n'a qu'un seul œil. Je ne finirois point, cher Yn-Che-Chan, si je te parlois de tous les Européens qui ont adopté cette fable. Si ce qu'ils disent étoit vrai, la moitié des humains n'auroient eu qu'un œil. Voici Solinus qui crée encore deux nouveaux peuples de Cyclopes. *Les Arimaspes,* dit-il, *qui demeurent aux environs de Besgulhra auprès de la mer Caspienne, n'ont qu'un œil.* Le même Auteur veut encore que dans les Indes il y ait des hommes qui n'ont qu'un œil & une jambe, & qui sont cependant très-legers & courent avec beaucoup de vitesse.

Ne sois point surpris, cher Yn-Che-Chan, de voir des Nations aussi mutilées que ces Indiennes, réduites à un seul œil & à une seule jambe, voici des peuples qui n'ont ni bouche ni langue; c'est bien-là un autre prodige, dont il est d'autant moins permis de douter, que plus de dix célébres Auteurs Européens en attestent l'authenticité. Pomponius Mela nous apprend qu'au-delà des déserts d'Egypte il y a plusieurs peuples muets: les uns ont une langue qui ne rend point de son, les autres sont sans langue; quelques-uns ont les levres jointes l'une contre l'autre, & n'ont qu'un petit trou sous le nez, qui sert de passage à l'eau que boivent ces peuples, & aux graines qu-ils

Solinus creates another nation of Cyclops, the Arimaspians, who inhabit those countries that border on the Caspian sea.
This author goes on to tell us of a people of India,
who have but one leg and one eye, and yet are extremely active, run with great swiftness, and live by hunting.

mangent. Nous venons de voir des Nations entieres métamorphosées en Cyclopes; en voilà actuellement d'autres changées en canaris & en chardonerets, à qui il ne reste au lieu de bouche, qu'un petit trou pour sifler & pour avaler quelques graines. Julius Solinus confirme cette respectable histoire, & Pline ne manque pas de l'autoriser, mais il va encore plus loin; car il veut que les Astromorres, peuple qui n' a point de bouche, ne se nourrissent que par le moyen de l'oderat. Voilà une Nation, chez laquelle une tulipe devoit valoir plus qu'un bœuf, & une violette plus qu'un mouton. Je m'étonne que Pline n'ait pas fait faire du miel aux Astromorres, puisqu'il les avoit changés en abeilles.

Mais voici de Nations bien plus extraordinaires que toutes celles dont nous venons de faire mention; elles sont composées d'hommes sans tête. Pomponius Mela écrit que les Blémiens n'en ont point, & que toutes les parties du visage sont attachées à la poitrine. Solinus assûre ce fait & le donne comme certain. Aulugelle raconte la même chose.

Le sort de ces hommes sans tête est bien moins triste, cher Yn-Che-Chan, que de ceux qui en avoient une de chien. Pline en donne une à tous les Cinamolgues, & il les fait aboyer, au lieu

. . . . but what would you say if you heard of men without any heads at all.[54] Pomponius Mela, Solinus, and Aulus Gellius, describe them to our hands: 'The Blemiae have a nose, eyes, and mouth on their breasts; or, as others will have it, placed in their shoulders.' . . .'[55] These people [the Arimaspians] we scarce know how to pity or admire; but the men whom Pliny calls Cynamolci, who have got the heads of dogs really deserves our compassion. Instead of language they express their sentiments by starting. Solinus confirms what

---

[54] The beginning of this passage is on p. 74, column 2, ll. 248-50.
[55] Continued p. 74, column 2, ll. 252-62.

de parler. Solinus adopte l'opinion des hommes chiens. Simon Mayole en parle amplement: a l'entendre parler, on diroit qu'il s'est entretenu familierement avec eux & qu'il entendoit parfaitement leur langage. *Lorsqu'on a passé*, dit-il, *les déserts de l'Egypte, on trouve les Cynocéphales qui habitent une contrée sur les frontieres de l'Ethiopie: ils vivent de dains & de bufles, ils n'ont point de voix, mais ils siflent; ils ont le menton si aigu, qu'on le prendroit pour le bout de la tête d'un serpent. Leurs mains sont armées de grands & longs ongles; leurs poitrine ressemble à celle des chiens barbets, ils sont très-legers à la course.* Qui croiroit, cher Yn-Che-Chan, que des gens semblables aux Cynocéphales fussent aussi délicats & eussent autant de vanité que des Mandarins Chinois, ou des Petits-Maîtres François? Cependant rien n'est si vrai, si nous ajoutons foi au même Auteur. *Les Cynocéphales*, dit-il, *ne refusent point de boire du vin, & mangent volontiers de la viande bouillie ou rotie. Ils aiment surtout que les mêts qu'on leur sert, soient bien apprêtés: s'ils sont mauvais ou peu délicats, ils s'en offensent; ils aiment fort aussi à être bien vêtus.* Voila, cher Yn-Che-Chan, des gens bien fiers. Je ne doute pas que si les grandes perruques Européennes eussent été à la mode du tems de Mayole, il

Pliny mentions, and Simon Mayole, a French bishop, talks of them as of particular and familiar acquaintances.

After passing the deserts of Egypt, says he, we meet with the Kunokeppaloi, who inhabit those regions that border on Ethiopia; they live by hunting; they cannot speak, but whistle; their chins resemble a serpent's head; their hands are armed with long sharp claws; their breast resembles that of a greyhound; and they excel in swiftness and agility.

Would you think it, my friend, that these odd kind of people are, notwithstanding their figure, excessively delicate; not even an alderman's wife, or a Chinese mandarine, can excel them in this particular.

These people, continues our faithful bishop, never refuse wine; love roast and boiled meat; they are particularly curious in having their meat well dressed, and spurn at it if in the least tainted.

n'eût coeffé magnifiquement toutes les têtes de chien des Cynocéphales; & pour quoi auroit-il fait quelque difficulté de les décorer en graves Sénateurs, puisque dans un autre endroit il les érige en maîtres de Rhétorique & en joueurs d'instrumens? *Lorsque les Ptolomées,* dit-il, *regnoient en Egypte, les Cynocéphales enseignoient les Lettres & à jouer de la flute.* Des joueurs de flute qui n'ont point de voix, & des maîtres de Grammaire qui ne parlent point, voilà de ces faits, cher Yn-Che-Chan, dignes d'être placés parmi les impertinences qu'ont écrites les disciples de *Foë* de leur chef & de leur Dieu. J'aime cependant beaucoup mieux les peuples de Simon Mayole, que ceux de Mela qui n'ont point absolument de tête.

Jusques ici nous avons vû des Nations estropiées & mutilées, nous leur en allons faire succéder d'autres, que seront aussi avantagées de la nature, que ces premières en étoient maltraitées. Mela donne à un peuple, qu'il place dans les isles Septentrionales, des oreilles qui sont d'une longueur si considérable, qu'ils n'ont pas besoin d'autres vêtemens pour se garantir des injures de l'air. Les tailleurs, cher Yn-Che-Chan, sont des gens inutiles chez ces Insulaires; ils se font des habits d'été & d'hyver avec

When the Ptolomies reigned in Egypt: (says he a little farther on) those men with dog's heads taught Grammar and Music. Men who had no voices to teach music, and who could not speak to teach Grammar, is, I confess, a little extraordinary.

Did ever the Disciples of Fohî broach any thing more ridiculous?

Hitherto we have seen men with heads strangely deformed, and with dog's heads. . . .[56]

One would think that these authors had an antipathy to the human form, and were resolved to make a new figure of their own: but let us do them justice, though they sometimes deprive us of a leg, an arm, an head, or some such trifling part of the body; they often as liberally bestow upon us something that we wanted before.[57]

[56] Continued p. 72, column 2, ll. 168-76.
[57] Continued from p. 72, column 2, l. 176.

leurs seules oreilles. Solinus donne aux Fanésiens des oreilles aussi avantageuses, & Pline habille & fournit de lit, par le moyen des mêmes oreilles, les habitans des isles Scythiques, peu éloignées du Royaume du Pont.

Les hommes aujourd'hui, cher Yn-Che-Chan, ne sont point assez heureux pour être aussi favorisés de la fortune ; les oreilles ne leur servent qu'à entendre, ils sont encore obligés de se chausser pour garantir leurs pieds des cailloux & des ronces. Mela a pourvû à cet inconvénient, en donnant des pieds de cheval aux Oones qui habitoient dans des isles Septentrionales. Solinus a rendu le même service aux Hipodes, & Pline a fait à ces deux peuples la même grace. Pausanias a eu la complaisance de métamorphoser tout un peuple en sapajoux, il l'a décoré d'une queue très-belle & très utile pour se garantir des mouches. Simon Mayole a aussi mis des queues aux Anglois : il prétend que plusieurs en avoient encore de son tems, & cet Auteur, qui vivoit il y a environ cent cinquante ans, & qui tenoit parmi les Pontifes Européens un rang distingué, n'en a pas moins écrit un mensonge aussi grossier. Voici les propres termes dont il se sert, *En Angleterre il y a des familles qui ont une queue, en punition de la moquerie & de la dérision que leurs peres firent d'un Augustin que St. Gregoire y avoit envoyé, & qui prêchoit en la*

Simon Mayole seems our particular friend in this particular : if he has denied heads to one part of mankind, he has given tails to another. He described many of the English of his time, which is not more than an hundred years ago, as having tails.

His own words are as follows.

In England there are some families which have tails, as a punishment for their deriding an Augustin Friar sent by S. Gregory, and who preached in Dorsetshire. They sewed, it seems, the

Dorocestrie, à la robe duquel ils attacherent des queues de grenouilles. Ajoutons foi aprés cela, cher Yn-Che-Chan, aux contes que nous débitent les Missionnaires, & à l'infaillibilité qu'ils accordent à leurs Pontifes. En voilà deux, dont l'un dit avoir vû en Ethiopie un peuple qui n'avoit qu'un œil, & l'autre assure que de son tems plusieurs personnes naissoient avec une queue en Angleterre, parce qu'ils s'étoient moqué d'un Augustin. C'est dommage que nos Bonses ne soient pas instruits à la Chine de ces belles histoires, ils en profiteroient sans doute, & donneroient des queues à ceux qui ne les respecteroient point.

Je ne finirois point, cher Yn-Che-Chan, si je voulois rapporter tous les mensonges, dont les Auteurs Européens ont rempli leurs livres au sujet de ces peuples imaginaires qui n'ont jamais existé. Il est vrai que depuis une centaine d'années les Ecrivains sont un peu plus retenus & respectent davantage leurs Lecteurs ; mais ils mentent cependant très-hardiment : & s'ils ne sont pas des hommes sans tête, n'ayant qu'une jambe, s'habillant avec leurs oreilles, &c. ils donnent aux Nations dont ils parlent, des mœurs, des loix, des usages si peu conformes à la vérité, qu' autant vaudroit-il

tails of different animals to his cloaths ; but soon they found those tails entailed on them and their posterity for ever. It is certain the author had some ground for this description ; many of the English wearing tails to their wigs to this very day, as a mark, I suppose, of the antiquity of their families, and perhaps as symbolical of those tails with which they were formerly distinguished by nature.

You see, my friend, there is nothing so ridiculous that has not at some time been said by some philosopher. The writers of books in Europe seem to think themselves authorized to say what they please ; an ingenious philosopher among them[58] has openly asserted, that he could persuade the whole republic of readers to believe the sun to be the cause neither of light nor heat ; if he could only get six philosophers on his side of the question.

Adieu."[59]

---

[58] Fontenelle.
[59] Goldsmith, *Chinese Letters,* No. XV.

qu'ils imitassent leurs prédeces-
seurs.

Dans la premiere Lettre que
je t'écrirai, cher Yn-Che-Chan,
je te prouverai, & te prouverai
invinciblement qu'il est impossible qu'il ait jamais existé aucun
de ces peuples, si différens de
ceux qui nous sont connus. Les
Chrétiens même semblent être
obligés par leur Religion à nier
qu'il y ait aucune réalité dans
ces fables absurdes, puisque les
hommes étant tous sortis du
premier qui fut formé par le
pouvoir divin, il est impossible
que ces races differentes aient
pû prendre naissance.

Porte-toi bien, cher Yn-Che-
Chan, & donne-moi, je te prie, de
tes nouvelles.[60]

I have chosen the above extracts as typical of three ways
in which Goldsmith borrowed from D'Argens. My quotations, however, constitute only a small portion of the cases
which are actual translations, or close paraphrases. I have
transcribed at sufficient length for the reader to be able to
observe his methods of rewriting and improving the
material of a less able writer; it remains only to be said
that there are, in all, ten letters from which borrowings are
of essentially the same character. The reader who cares to
examine them will find them listed below.[61] Attention is

[60] D'Argens, *Lettres Chinoises* 2. 25-37.
[61] The references below are to *The Citizen of the World*, ed. Gibbs.
Letter IV (3. 21): The first sentence of the essay is modeled on
Let. Chin., Lettre I (1. 2,), beginning of the third paragraph.

Letter IX (3. 36): The remarks on prostitutes which form the
second paragraph of the letter are translated from D'Argens' Lettre
XXI (1. 208-210). England is substituted for France as the country
involved.

called to the fact that Goldsmith's use of the *Lettres Chinoises* began even before the first numbered letter in the *Public Ledger*. After the sixty-fifth newspaper letter, he ceased to make textual borrowings; but, since we know the extent to which he had already depended upon the *Lettres Chinoises,* other close resemblances deserve citation, which under different circumstances would be unwarranted.

For example, Letter XXXVI of the *Lettres Chinoises* possibly suggested a topic for satire with which Goldsmith was already familiar; so by changing the scene from France to England he had a subject to hand, which could easily be amplified from his own experience. In this case the topic

Letter X (3. 38-40): With the exception of the introductory paragraph and of a few scattered sentences, the whole letter—a description of the customs and religion of the Daures—is translated from D'Argens' Lettre XXVIII (1. 293-301).

Letter XII (3. 44-45): The account of English deathbed customs in paragraphs two to six is a slightly rearranged translation of bits of Lettres V and VI of D'Argens (1. 40-2, 45-7), where, however. the allusion is to France.

Letter XVI (3. 58-62): The whole letter—on the accounts of fabulous people to be found in European historical writings—is a considerably condensed translation of *Let. Chin.* XXXI (2. 25-37).

Letter XIX (3. 72): The next to the last paragraph is taken from *Let. Chin.* XLII (2. 153-4), where it forms part of a long development on Russian marriage customs.

Letter XLIII (3. 161-3): The opening passage on the loss suffered by humanity in the death of a philosopher is constructed out of two short developments in *Let. Chin.* LXXXIV (3. 306 ff.).

Letter LXIV (3. 240-1): The discussion of European titles in the first paragraph is a translation of the first two paragraphs of *Let. Chin.* LXV (3. 76-7).

Letter CXVIII (3. 425-7): The whole account of Fum Hoam's experiences in Japan is a somewhat condensed translation of *Let. Chin.* CXXV (5. 81 ff.). D'Argens' account is derived from Kaempfer's *History of Japan* 2. 529 ff.

This note is quoted from *A French Influence on Goldsmith's Citizen of the World,* by Donald S. Crane and the present writer, which appeared in *Modern Philology*, Vol. 19, No. 1, August, 1921.

was the lack of respect paid to philosophers. A brief quotation will illustrate D'Argens' treatment of it. D'Argens' Chinese philosopher, entering a church in Paris, was attracted by a tomb, the grandeur of which pointed to the fact that it must be the resting place of a man who had rendered singular service to his country or to civilization. He at once jumped to the conclusion that it was the tomb of Descartes, and, seeing a native standing by, the Oriental demanded if that were the case. His guide replied thus:

> Vous prenez cette status pour celle de Descartes? C'est celle d'un Cardinal Italien, dont l'avarice & l'ambition ont mis plusieurs fois le Royaume à deux doigts de sa perte. Ha vraiment, ce Descartes dont vous parlez, a bien un tombeau somme celui-là, dont la plus petite partie à plus couté à construire, que tous les hommes de Lettres à enterrer depuis l'origine du monde? Ce Philosophe a pour toute marque de distinction, une inscription attachée contra la muraille d'une Eglise: un savetier qui fonde pour quinze écus un service annual est traité aussi honorablement.[62]

In the *Chinese Letters,* Letter XII, Goldsmith copied D'Argens to this extent. His Chinese wanderer likewise entered a church, Westminster Abbey, and was attracted by the monuments to the dead. Noticing that a foreigner was admiring these tombs, a gentleman, the Man-in-Black, approached him, and offered his services to explain their significance. The Chinese, seeing a monument of superior excellence, suggested that it must be 'a trophy raised to the memory of some king who has saved his country from ruin,' or to one who had done some other service to his country. The Man-in-Black contradicted this opinion. The Chinese then demanded for what the man who was buried here was remarkable. 'Remarkable, sir! ... why, sir, the gentleman

---

[62] D'Argens, *Lettres Chinoises* 2. 88.

that lies here is remarkable, very remarkable for a tomb in Westminster-abbey.[63] Goldsmith continues to elaborate the absurdity of burying certain men in the Abbey, and to explain the injustice done to great men by having no tomb, where they deserved one. The topic of this essay, which might seem to have arisen from the casual observations of the day was, I think, undoubtedly suggested by the brief remarks of D'Argens.

Other examples of resemblances between the two works which do not involve direct textual borrowings are numerous. I list them below.[64]

[63] Goldsmith, *Chinese Letters*, No. XII, *Public Ledger*, February 25, 1760; *The Citizen of the World*, Letter XIII.

[64] Letters I and II: Lien Chi Altangi is befriended by merchants at Amsterdam. Compare *Let. Chin.* I (1. 3 ff.).

Letter II (3. 15): Coaches blocking up the streets of London. Cf. the description of the same phenomenon in Paris in *Let. Chin.* I (1. 7-8).

Letter III (3. 18): Criticism of the notion that the strangeness of European customs implies a departure from 'nature.' Cf. *Let. Chin.* LIII (2. 276-7) and, for the details, XXVIII (1. 301-6) and XXX (2. 15-16).

Letter III (3. 19-20): Comparison of English and Chinese fine ladies. Cf. *Let. Chin.* II (1. 10-2) and IV (1. 33-4).

Letter VI (3. 29): 'Tien, the universal soul.' Cf. *Let. Chin.* XLIV (2. 175), and *passim.*

Letter X (3. 89): 'The sectaries of Fohi.' D'Argens, from whom the context is translated, has 'Lao-Kium' (1. 296). But cf. *Let. Chin.* XI (1. 94-105).

Letter XIII (3. 48): A 'gentleman dressed in black,' with whom Lien Chi discusses the monuments in Westminster Abbey. D'Argens, in Lettre LVIII (3. 1-11), describes a conversation in a Paris book-shop between Sioeu-Tcheou and 'un homme habillé de noir.'

Letter XV (3. 57): 'One of their doctors.' Probably an allusion to the unnamed Jesuit, whose theories concerning the souls of animals D'Argens summarized in Lettre LIV (2. 289-292).

Letter XIX (3. 71): ' "Psha man," replied he, smiling; . . . . "one half of the kingdom would flog the other." ' Cf., for a similar remark in a similar context, *Let. Chin.* XLIII (2. 170).

Goldsmith's indebtedness to D'Argens was great. At a time when the young journalist was finding it hard to get under way his new venture in the *Public Ledger,* much of his writing was derivative. But as the months went on, Goldsmith found it no longer necessary to consult the writings of others; for rather than strive to fill his letters

Letter XXXIII (3. 126) : English comments on Lien Chi's personal appearance. Cf. *Let. Chin.* I (1. 4-5).

Letter XXXIII (3. 128) : Lien Chi's familiarity with factors and missionaries in China. Cf. *Let. Chin.* VII (1. 55).

Letter XXXVII (3. 138) : 'An ancient Guebre of the number, remarkable for his piety and wisdom.' Cf. D'Argens' account of the virtues of the Guebres, *Let. Chin.* CV (4. 196-7).

Letter XLII (3. 157-8) : Contrast between the stability of China, with her policy of toleration, and the anarchy of Europe, torn by revolutions and religious wars. Cf. *Let. Chin.* VIII (1. 70-3), and LII (2. 266 ff.).

Letter LI (3. 191-5) : A conversation between Lien Chi and a bookseller. There are two such conversations in D'Argens; see *Let. Chin.* XXIX (3. 1-14) and LVIII (3. 1-11).

Letter LVI (3. 211) : Description of the state of Russia. Apparently summarized from *Let. Chin.* XXXV (2. 71) and LVII (2. 322 ff.).

Letter LVI (3. 211-2) : Description of the German Empire. Apparently a generalization from *Let. Chin.* XCIV (4. 74-83) and XCV (4. 83-93).

Letter LVI (3. 212) : Description of Sweden. Cf. D'Argens' account of Denmark in Lettre CXXII (5. 42-53). It is significant that the *Public Ledger* text reads: 'Sweden . . . is probably (like Denmark of late) only hastening on to despotism' (3. 212, note). The words in parenthesis were omitted from the collected edition of 1762.

Letter XCIX, *Public Ledger* text (3. 363, note) : 'Hyde rel. Pers.' There are many references to Hyde in D'Argens; see Tome IV, *passim.*

Letter CXI (3. 400) : 'Talapoins.' D'Argens gives an account of the 'Talapoins' in Tome V, *passim.*

This note is reprinted with changed references from *A French Influence on Goldsmith's Citizen of the World,* by Donald S. Crane and the present writer. See *Mod. Phil.* Vol. 19, No. 1, August, 1921.

with Oriental material with which he first had to familiarize himself, he wrote of English manners and customs, satirized the foibles of his own nation, and only infrequently made use of source-books when it was necessary to recall Eastern background. In writing kindly of human faults, Goldsmith needed no aid.

6. 1757. WALPOLE, HORATIO. *A Letter from Xo-Ho, a Chinese Philosopher at London, to his friend Lien Chi at Peking, 1757.*

Horace Walpole's Letter from Xo-Ho, which was written on May 12, 1757, went through five editions in a fortnight. It sold for the small sum of sixpence. Writing as Xo-Ho, Walpole satirized the politics of a nation which would allow such gross injustice as the recent execution of Admiral Byng. Through Oriental eyes, the Chinese traveler in England sees the absurdity of the British method of making ministers, the ridiculous contention of the two existing political parties, and the unfortunate split of the government into three factions.

Although Walpole's short tract concerned itself chiefly with politics, there is also satire on English weather, on English dress, and on the foibles of English society and character.

The immense popularity which caused the Letter from Xo-Ho to run through five editions in two weeks, was a good indication of the possible success of a prolonged series of letters of the same kind. It must have encouraged Goldsmith to entertain such a scheme. Walpole, in fact, throws out a hint of the interest which such a series would command, by referring to certain past letters of Xo-Ho, thus pretending that his own tract was one of a series written by the Chinese.

The name Lien Chi, used by Goldsmith for his philosophic wanderer, was in all probability taken from *The Letter from Xo-Ho to his friend Lien Chi at Peking.*

7. 1756. *Letter from an Armenian in Ireland, to his Friends at Trebisonde, &c. Translated in the Year 1756.*[65]

The *Letters from an Armenian in Ireland,* a series of pseudo-letters from an Armenian traveling abroad to his various friends at Trebizond, appeared in 1756. The authorship of the anonymous volume in which they were printed is still under dispute. These letters are satirical in character; they deal with the politics of Ireland; they tell of the government of that land; they describe and characterize its inhabitants; and they criticize its moral and social institutions.

Although these letters did not contribute any definite or specific material to Goldsmith's *Chinese Letters,* they did influence that composition in a negative way. By reading this volume Goldsmith estimated its values, and established a critical basis upon which he was able to formulate a judgment of how to compose his own pseudo-letters, when he came to write them.

What this judgment was, may best be illustrated by quoting Goldsmith's review of the *Letters from an Armenian in Ireland.* This account, which appeared in the *Monthly Review,* August, 1757, runs in part as follows:

> The Writer who would inform, or improve, his countrymen, under the assumed character of an Eastern Traveller, should be careful to let nothing escape him which might betray the imposture. If his aim is satirical, his remarks should be collected from the more striking follies abounding in the country he describes,

[65] 'In the title of the British Museum copy, is written, "by Judge H-l-n"; and the Museum catalogue has "[By R. Hellen?]." R. Hellen was a judge of Common Pleas in Ireland. . . . In Halkett and Laing's Dict. Anon., &c., Literature, vol. ii, 1883, the Armenian Letters (dated 1757) are attributed to Edm. Sexton Pery.' Goldsmith, *Works,* ed. Gibbs, 3. 285, note 1.

and from those prevailing absurdities which commonly usurp the softer name of fashions. His accounts should be of such a nature, as we may fancy his Asiatic friend would wish to know,—such as we ourselves would expect from a Correspondent in Asia.

Whether the country our Author describes was deficient in materials, and had not national follies enough for general satire, we are not to determine; but certain it is, he has by no means been cautious in his endeavours to preserve the fictitious character he has assumed. This pretended Armenian espouses party, enters into the minutiæ of the politics of Ireland, explains Poynings Act, and pays not a little attention to my Lady Mayoress, the Chandler's daughter. While these, and topics more trifling than these, make up the correspondence, in vain is every period stiffened with *thee* and *thou;* in vain does he swear, or pray, like a zealous Mussulman. . . .

But tho' this performance contains little that can be supposed to excite the curiosity of an inhabitant of Trebisonde, (and is, consequently, in this respect defective) it contains many things interesting to a native of Britain.[66]

In composing the *Chinese Letters*, Goldsmith did his best to apply the critical principles which he advances here with such care. In the first place, he took every opportunity of keeping up the versimilitude of their authorship. In the second place, he made it a practice throughout the *Public Ledger* essays to satirize native 'follies' and 'prevailing absurdities which commonly usurp the softer names of fashions,' rather than expose the more serious vices and evils which are obviously wrong, and common to *all* mankind. Again, he made it a principle to avoid the narrow squabbles of political parties, and personal gossip, endeavoring to confine himself entirely to national and human interests. And, once more, he established the rule of

---

[66] *Monthly Review,* August, 1757, pp. 150-1.

avoiding the ornate and pompous style which contemporary critics called 'Eastern.' In the *Chinese Letters,* Letter XXXI[67] (April 25, 1760), he refers, as he does in this review, to the error into which the imitators of Eastern style fall by the unnatural use of *thee* and *thou.*

CHAPTER VI

THE SOURCES: GROUP B.

Works not on the plan of *The Citizen of the World,* which were used by Goldsmith for concrete material.

1. LE COMTE, LOUIS. *Memoirs and Observations ... Made in a late Journey Through the Empire of China.*[1]

Le Comte's *Memoirs and Observations* served Goldsmith for a reference-book. From it, and from Père Du Halde's *General History,* he took the majority of the facts concerning Chinese life with which he filled the columns of the *Public Ledger.* It is practicable to record here only the more important points, and to indicate in general how Goldsmith used the book. Further details have a more appropriate place in an appendix.

[67] *The Citizen of the World,* Letter XXXIII.
[1] *Memoirs and\ Observations Topographical, Physical, Mathematical, Mechanical, Natural, Civil, and Ecclesiastical. Made in a late Journey Through the Empire of China, and Published in several Letters.* By Louis Le Comte Jesuit. *Translated from the Paris Edition. ...* The Second Edition very much corrected. ... London, 1698. Translated from: *Nouveaux Mémoires sur l' Etat Présent de la Chine. Par le P. Louis Le Comte de la Compagnie de Jesus, Mathématicien au Roy a Paris,* 1696. The English translation is quoted, because careful comparison of the English and French versions with the *Chinese Letters* shows that Goldsmith undoubtedly used the former. Also one passage used by Goldsmith comes from the preface to the translation, which did not appear in the French original.

In the pages of Le Comte are many descriptions of Chinese conventions, which Goldsmith copied when he composed his *Chinese Letters*. For example, there is an explanation of the Eastern conception of personal beauty. This demands abnormally long finger-nails, since thus the high-born are distinguished from those employed in the mechanical arts; and the wrapping of the feet of wealthy females, in order that they may be differentiated from those who, by reason of their poverty, must use their feet for walking. There is an account of a Chinese call. There are other descriptions, given by Le Comte, of curiosities, such as the native goldfish which ornament the pools of courts and gardens among the great, of the Gin Sem[2] which is used as a simple, of mourning costumes, which are white, instead of black, among the Chinese, and of gambling, which prevails among the common people and gentry alike, to such an extent that the latter often hazard their estates, their houses, and even their wives and children, upon the turn of a single card. Then there are descriptions of the Feast of Lanthorns, of the practices of the heretical sect of idolators who worship the God Fohi, and of the odd signboards which many placed before their shops. Of all these things Goldsmith made use.[3] Detail of this kind gave the impression that the author was a *bona fide* Chinese.

Further use of the *Memoirs and Observations* is found in the quotations of the maxims of Confucius. It was Goldsmith's custom to enforce the moral of his essays by citing a Chinese precept, which he did not take from the authentic works of Confucius, but copied from the accounts of the Jesuit. Although he gives direct reference to the Latin

[2] From which comes the English *ginseng*.

[3] The page-references for the above mentioned descriptions are given in the appendix, pp. 148 ff.

edition[4] of these works, careful searching of its pages has revealed the fact that the reference was professional *hocus pocus*. Goldsmith took several of these proverbs from the list which Le Comte designates by the following:

> The Maxims of Morality he [Confucius] hath scattered here and there in his Works.... There would need an entire Volume to relate them all. I have taken the few following out of a Book composed by one of the principal *Mandarins* of the Empire, who rules in Pekin.[5]

In choosing this work, it will be noticed that Goldsmith used the book nearest at hand. He took the easiest way, because his purpose was only to give an appearance of Orientalism.

From this list in the *Memoirs and Observations*, Goldsmith copied the following maxims:

Le Comte, Maxim III. A Man ought to change often, if he would be constant in Wisdom.[6]

Goldsmith. *They must often change, says Confucius, who would be constant in happiness or wisdom.*[7]

Le Comte, Maxim X. One ought not to wonder that the wise Man walks slower in the way of Vertue, than the ill Man does in that of Vice, Passion hurries, and Wisdom guides.[8]

Goldsmith. *We are not to be astonished, says Confucius, that the wise walk more slowly in their road to virtue, than*

---

[4] *Confucius Sinarum Philosophus, sine Scientia Sinensis Latine exposita.* ... P. Couplet, Paris, 1687.

[5] *Memoirs and Observations*, pp. 201-2.

[6] *Memoirs and Observations*, p. 203.

[7] *Chinese Letters*, Letter CXVI; *The Citizen of the World*, Letter CXXIII.

[8] *Memoirs and Observations*, p. 207.

fools in their passage to vice; since passion drags us along, while wisdom only points out the way.[9]

Le Comte, Maxim XII. In the State wherein we are, Perseverance in Well-doing consists not so much in not falling, as in rising again as often as we fall.[10]

Goldsmith. *True magnanimity consists not in NEVER falling, but in RISING every time we fall.*[11]

Besides frequently consulting Le Comte for the purpose of supplying the detail for the Oriental setting, Goldsmith collected from the *Memoirs and Observations* numerous anecdotes for an essay to show that the history of the rulers of China is more replete with great actions than the history of Western sovereigns. This essay, Letter XLI, in the *Public Ledger,* appeared on May 30, 1760.[12] In it Fum Hoam says: 'Upon opening the Chinese history, I there beheld an antient extended empire, established by laws which nature and reason seem to have dictated.' The source of Fum Hoam's reference, which seems to allude to history in general, rather than to any specific work of history, has been overlooked by Goldsmith's editors. The passages which follow, however, identify it with the *Memoirs and Observations,* and throw considerable light on the long debated question of Goldsmith's Chinese information.

[9] *Chinese Letter,* Letter LIII. Goldsmith acknowledges the source of this quotation in a note: 'Tho' this fine maxim be not found in the Latin edition of the morals of Confucius, yet we find it ascribed to him by Le Comte.' The above mentioned letter is in *The Citizen of the World,* Letter LVI.

[10] *Memoirs and Observations,* p. 208.

[11] *Chinese Letters,* Letter XXI; *The Citizen of the World,* Letter XXII. Goldsmith also used this proverb in an earlier letter in *The Citizen of the World,* first edition, 1762, Letter VII, p. 22, where it reads: 'Our greatest glory is, not in never falling, but in rising every time we fall.' The proverb does not appear, however, in the letter corresponding in the *Chinese Letters.*

[12] *The Citizen of the World,* Letter XLII.

In the Chapter 'Of the Policy and Government of the Chinese,' Père Le Comte relates at length the extraordinary value which the state sets upon obedience of children to their parents. This obedience, he says, is the strength of the Chinese nation; for the people are merely the children of the state, and the emperor is the servant of the people.[13] This idea Goldsmith makes the moral issue of his essay. 'The duty of children to their parents, a duty which nature implants in every breast,' he puts it, 'forms the strength of that government which has subsisted for time immemorial. Filial obedience is the first and greatest requisite of a state; by this we become good subjects of our emperors, capable of behaving with just subordination to our superiors, and grateful dependants on heaven.'[14] These statements are an epitome of the historian's account of the policy and government of China.[15]

Of course Le Comte employs divers anecdotes in proof of his point. Goldsmith selects from these to reinforce his argument. The first of them is a story of twelve mandarins who suffered death for venturing to offer advice to a tyrant. and who, by their courage and obedience in submitting to the sentence, reclaimed their sovereign to leniency.[16] The account of Goldsmith is much shorter than that of Le Comte. What the latter says in four paragraphs, the former says in half a paragraph. The condensation is brought about by the omission of detail in describing the actions of each mandarin as he presented himself before the emperor. The tyrant is referred to by Le Comte as 'one of our emperors,' while Goldsmith specifies him by the name

[13] *Memoirs and Observations*, pp. 270, 277.

[14] *Chinese Letters*, Letter XLI; *The Citizen of the World*, Letter XLII.

[15] *Memoirs and Observations*, Part II: 'Of the Policy and Government of the Chinese.'

[16] *Works* 3. 158.

Tisiang. The moral drawn, and the purpose of including the anecdote, are the same in both authors.

A second anecdote of this character, which immediately follows the story of the twelve mandarins, is taken, not from Le Comte, but from Du Halde's *General History*.[17]

A third example illustrative of the great actions of Chinese sovereigns concerns the emperor who, betrayed by his subjects, entered his garden, killed his little daughter, and then, before taking his own life, spoke these words: *Forsaken by my subjects, abandoned by my friends, use my body as you will, but spare, O spare, my people.*[18] Goldsmith has only slightly condensed; the details remain identical. Undoubtedly he saw this story in Le Comte, but it is more likely that he rewrote it from Du Halde, where it also appears;[19] the name of the emperor given by Du Halde, and used by Goldsmith, is not mentioned in the *Memoirs and Observations*.

The essay is brought to a close with the observation that the greatness of the country is derived from its hardihood in long withstanding the invasions of the Tartars, and in its ultimate refusal to admit the ancient enemy into the empire. The facts which support this observation are also found in the source.

It was Goldsmith's aim in the *Chinese Letters* to instruct his nation by example. In these anecdotes from the history of China, the reader will recognize a favorite thesis of the author of *The Traveller* and *The Deserted Village*: luxury softens a people, and causes national demoralization; hardships develop individual manliness, which is the strength of

---

[17] The anecdote is discussed below, p. 100.

[18] *Chinese Letters*, Letter XLI; *The Citizen of the World*, Letter XLII. Le Comte's account of the story is to be found in the *Memoirs and Observations*, p. 18. Le Comte writes: 'My Subjects have basely forsaken me, spend thy Rage on my Body, but spare my People.'

[19] See below, p. 101.

any government. I find that in searching for Oriental background, Goldsmith frequently ran across material which supported preconceived ideas of his own, and which for this reason he used. In other cases, as exemplified in examples of detail concerning Chinese affairs, he went in definite search of Oriental material to establish an already determined topic.

The preface to *The Citizen of the World*, which was, of course, written for the first collected edition of the *Chinese Letters*, contains another brief specimen taken from Le Comte. Here, however, Goldsmith acknowledges his source in a footnote, which reads, 'Le Comte vol. 1, p. 210.' The text to which this note refers reads in Goldsmith, '*How comes it*, said they, *that the Europeans, so remote from China, think with so much justice and precision? They have never read our books, they scarcely know even our letters, and yet they talk and reason just as we do.*'[20] This idea is expressed by Le Comte in the following words: 'But perceiving the *Europeans* instructed in all sorts of Sciences, they the Chinese were struck with Astonishment. *How can it possibly be,* said they, *that a People so far remote from us, should have any Wit or Capacity? They have never perused our Books; they were never modelled by our Laws, and yet they speak, discourse, and argue aright as we do.*'[21] By these words each author aims to show, as Goldsmith puts it, that 'the truth is, the Chinese and we are pretty much alike. Different degrees of refinement, and not of distance, mark the distinctions among mankind.'[22]

The discovery that human nature is much the same in every country, that national differences lie in superficialities, rather than in fundamental emotions of the heart, was a principle which Goldsmith learned early from his Conti-

---

[20] *The Citizen of the World*, ed. 1762.
[21] *Memoirs and Observations*, ed. 1698, p. 121.
[22] *The Citizen of the World*, ed. 1762.

nental travels. Because he had acquired this cosmopolitan understanding, he felt equipped to show in random articles, in *The Traveller,* and in *The Citizen of the World,* its importance to the Englishman, who, less fortunate than himself, had not made the grand tour.

2. Du Halde. *The General History of China.*[23]

The most important source of Goldsmith's knowledge of the Orient and of his exotic allusions is Du Halde's *General History of China.*[24] In its pages, even more than in the pages of Le Comte's earlier *Memoirs and Observations,* he found material for his Eastern coloring. In order to make the English believe that the author of the *Chinese Letters* was a Chinese, familiar mention of details of Chinese daily life was necessary. By casual reference to the gods and kings of China, to anecdotes of the great men, to the pastimes and occupations of the people, and to stories from their literature, he gave a setting to his story. With names of provinces, cities, rivers, and mountains, he attempted to add conviction of the reality of his picture, through concrete allusion. As Goldsmith had no knowledge of these matters, he was dependent upon reference-books for his information.

In the pages of Du Halde's history Goldsmith found much that was of use. In them are the stories that Fo, or Fohi, was the founder of the Chinese monarchy; that Tien,

---

[23] Du Halde, *The General History of China. Containing a Geographical, Historical, Chronological, Political and Physical Description of the Empire of China, Chinese-Tartary, Corea, and Thibet. Including an Exact and Particular Account of their Customs, Manners, Ceremonies, Religion, Arts and Sciences. The Whole adorn'd with Curious Maps, and Variety of Copper-Plates. Done from the French of P. Du Halde.* London, 1736.

[24] Goldsmith used the English translation of Du Halde's *Description géographique, historique, chronologique, politique, et physique de l'empire de la Chine.* . . . La Haye, 1696.

which signifies at once emperor and Supreme Being, was
the spirit which presides over Heaven; and that Yu and
Tching ting vang (whom Goldsmith calls Chinvang the
Chaste) were notable sovereigns of famous dynasties.
There also the information is given that Maccau, or Macao,
was the port of the province of Ouang Tchen, and that
Honan (the district in which Lien Chi Altangi resided)
was noted for the mildness of its climate and the fertility
of its soil. Again, in this place he was informed concerning
the dogma of the three religious sects of China, of the
material in the Books of *the Ceremonies,* and of the three
souls of Fohi.

Du Halde's work, too, told him of Eastern myth. It
described the *Fong Hoang* as a rare fictitious bird (much
like the Phœnix) resembling an eagle, and excelling him in
the great variety of his colors. Imitations of this *fong
whang,* as Goldsmith calls it, were used as head-dresses of
ladies. The herb *gin seng,* so often alluded to in the
Chinese Letters, is described by Du Halde, as well as the
goldfish kept by persons of distinction in garden basins.
Again, accounts of eating strange foods, such as bears'
claws, are retailed by the Jesuit, and recounted by Goldsmith as an exotic custom. The strange Chinese standard
of beauty which is mentioned by Le Comte, and often
referred to by Goldsmith, is emphasized by Du Halde in this
way: 'That which they [the Chinese] chiefly admire, as
making a perfect Beauty, is a large Forehead, short Nose,
small Eyes, a Visage large and square, broad and large
Ears, a Mouth middle sized, and the Hair black, for they
cannot bear to see it yellow or red; however, there must be
a certain Symmetry and Proportion between all the Parts
to render them agreeable.'[25]

These minor details, which occur in both Du Halde and
Goldsmith, are important. Their use illustrates clearly

---

[25] *General History* 2. 138.

Goldsmith's method of writing. He simply turned the pages of the two most accessible histories, and looked up his facts. Then he used them, hoping to convince his public of the Chinese nationality of the author of the *Chinese Letters*. From these two accounts almost every Chinese reference in the pages of *The Citizen of the World* can be annotated.[26]

The longer passages in Du Halde which contributed numerous essays of the *Chinese Letters* are perhaps as important, in revealing Goldsmith's method, as the accumulation of details cited above. Letter XVII of the *Chinese Letters*[27] contains the first of these.

This letter, which appeared in the *Public Ledger* on March 15, 1760, relates the story of Choang and Hansi, a tale revealing the insincerity of effusive affection; it is a variant of the familiar story of the Matron of Ephesus.[28] There can be little doubt that Goldsmith took it from the *General History*. There it appears as a Chinese novel (of which Du Halde gives the translation, with the titles: *Tchoang tse, after the Funeral Obsequies of his Wife, wholly addicts himself to his beloved Philosophy, and becomes famous among the Sect of Tao.*[29] The preface to the tale by the Chinese writer points the same moral as does Goldsmith's preface to his version of the story. In his

[26] Specific comparison of examples omitted here may be found in the appendix to Du Halde, pp. 191-215, where many of the more important examples are given.

[27] *The Citizen of the World*, Letter XVIII.

[28] Cf. note to Letter XVIII 'in Dobson's edition of *The Citizen of the World* (op. cit., p. 182, n.) ; W. Seele: *Voltaire's Zadig* (op. cit., p. 128) ; and K. Campbell: *The Seven Sages of Rome* . . . . Boston, 1907, Introduction, pp. ci-cviii, which gives seventy-six derivatives and analogues of the story known as *Vidua*, of which the *Matron of Ephesus* is the most famous version.'—Conant, *The Oriental Tale in England*, p. 194.

[29] *General History* 3. 134.

account, Goldsmith compares the effusive affection and passionate outbursts of English married couples to the moderation of conduct in wedlock among the Dutch. He emphasizes the insincerity of extravagant endearments, and the danger of unrestrained passion. Likewise the Chinese writer warns his readers. He says: 'My only Design is to shew that we ought to be careful in distinguishing between true and false Merit, in order to regulate our Affections; and as it is very dangerous to be a Slave to a blind Passion, it is likewise of great consequence to our Repose to keep within the Bounds of Moderation; generally speaking, those who constantly strive to subdue their Passions will at length become Masters; then Wisdom will be their Portion, and a calm and serene Life will be the Fruit of their Labour.'[30]

The story which follows this moralizing introduction is much the same in both accounts. The first four pages of the historian's narrative deal with the life and philosophic training of Tchoang tse, the future law-giver, who, it is carefully explained, was brought up in the doctrines of Lao. This portion of the account, which is in no way connected with the actual story of conjugal love, is omitted by Goldsmith, who begins his narration at once; yet the facts in it were known to the English author, for he refers to 'Choang, who had early been taught wisdom in the school of Lao,' and he mentions Choang as 'the law-giver.' From this point on, the facts and the details of the two versions are similar, although in some minor matters Goldsmith has made slight alterations. A comparison of the episodes of the two versions will illustrate the closeness of the parallel:

[30] *General History* 3. 135.

The *Novel*
(Translated by Du Halde)

1. Life and education of Tchou-ang.

2. Tchouang meets the widow who is fanning the grave of her husband, in order that she may obey his dying injunction not to marry while his grave is still wet.

3. Tchouang discovers his wife directly behind him, and relates to her the story of the widow, saying he fears similar treatment in case of his death.

4. Tien (Tchouang's wife) scolds the widow for her insensibility, and flies into a rage at the suggestion of her husband, swearing fidelity.

5. Tchuang taken sick, appears to be dead, and is placed in a coffin.

6. An old disciple of Tchouang's comes to the funeral.

7. A servant tells Tien that the Disciple is in love with her, and is set on by Tien to argue his master into marrying her.

8. The Disciple and Tien agree to marry.

9. The apartments are decorated for the wedding ceremony.

10. The bridegroom falls sick of a disease which can be cured only by drinking the brain of a man newly killed.

11. Tien demands whether the brain of a man who died a natural death would do.

Goldsmith
(Story of Choan and Hansi)

1. Omitted by Goldsmith.

2. Choang meets the widow under similar circumstances.

3. Choang brings the widow home, and relates her story to his wife, saying he fears similar treatment in case of his death.

4. Hansi (Choang's wife) is angered at her husband's suggestion, and drives the widow from her doors, swearing fidelity to Choang.

5. An old disciple of Choang's comes to dinner at Choang's, and the husband and wife show open signs of affection, forgetting the quarrel.

6. Choang falls into an apoletic fit, appearing dead.

7. Omitted by Goldsmith.

8. The Disciple and Hansi agree to marry.

9. The apartments are decorated for the wedding ceremony.

10. The bridegroom falls sick of a disease which can be cured only by the application of the heart of a man newly killed.

11. Hansi demands whether the heart of a man lately dead would do.

12. Tien breaks open with an axe her husband's coffin, in order to obtain his brains.

13. Tchouang comes to life, and discovers his wife's infidelity.

14. Tien hangs herself, because of mortification.

15. Tchouang resolves never to marry again, and, joining his Master, Lao, ends his days with the comforts of philosophy.

12. Hansi breaks open with an axe her husband's coffin, in order to obtain his heart.

13. Choang comes to life, and discovers his wife's infidelity.

14. Hansi stabs herself, because of mortification.

15. Choang marries the widow with the large fan.

The close resemblance of the stories is clear from the above. It will be observed that the name of the husband Tchouang, used in the Chinese history, is merely a different spelling of the name Choang, used by Goldsmith. The name of the wife in the novel was Tien; in Goldsmith's essay it became Hansi. In the original Tien hanged herself; in the English version she stabbed herself. In the original, Tchouang, after coming back to life, and learning the infidelity of his wife, vowed eternal celibacy, met with his master Lao, and spent his declining days in philosophy; in the Goldsmith version, he married the widow who dried the grave of her husband with a large fan. The moral purpose of both endings is the same. The former is entirely serious; the latter, while quite as serious, adds the touch of humor. Goldsmith puts it: 'Choang, being a philosopher, was too wise to make any loud lamentations; he thought it best to bear his loss with serenity; so, mending up the old coffin where he had lain himself, he placed his faithless spouse in his room; and, unwilling that so many nuptial preparations should be expended in vain, the same night married the widow with the large fan.'[31] And here follows the moral point of the essay. In such statements, not in the supposed erudition of his Chinese knowledge, is found

[31] *Chinese Letters*, Letter XVII; *The Citizen of the World*, Letter XVIII.

the wisdom, not the learning, of Goldsmith: 'As they both were apprised of the foibles of each other before-hand, they knew how to excuse them after marriage. They lived together for many years in great tranquility, and not expecting rapture, found content.'[32] The above treatment of the story is a good single example of the results gained by Goldsmith's method of handling sources. Du Halde wrote the story in twenty-one pages; Goldsmith told it in three. Goldsmith always omitted useless details. In this case he did not adopt the phraseology of Du Halde; he merely read over the Chinese novel, and retold it in his own words. To the purely moralistic or pedantic writings of other authors he added in this, as in every case, the touch of real humor, the influence of his own personality, and a real knowledge of and sympathy with human weakness.

Goldsmith again shows his insight into the foibles of human character in the *Chinese Letters,* Letter XXXVIII.[33] He found the material once more in the pages of the *General History.* Du Halde, in the second volume of this work, describes at length the various exaggerated ceremonies connected with Chinese salutations, visits, letters, marriages, and funerals. Since the description of these exotic ceremonies would be interesting to the London public, Goldsmith included them. But this was not the only reason for his doing so; artificiality and insincerity of fashion always appealed to his genially humorous and mildly moralizing pen. From Du Halde's account of the ceremonies, he selected the description of a suitor's call, for the topic of an essay which might be summarized by the following sentence: 'Ceremonies are different in every country, but true politeness is everywhere the same.'[34] The point which Goldsmith made was, in other words, that true gentility does not consist merely in fashionable behavior. In order to

---

[32] *Ibid.*

[33] *The Citizen of the World,* Letter XXXIX.

[34] *Ibid.*

illustrate this point, he submits two letters; one from a lady who leads the fashion in England, the other from a lady who 'sets the ceremonies of China.' It is then left to the reader to decide whether the actions of these ladies, on receiving their suitors, although they vary in detail according to the differences in national custom, are not in reality equally blameworthy because of their insincerity.

Du Halde points out that good Chinese manners on the occasion of a formal call are judged by

> The Number of Bows that you are to make, the Terms you are to make use of, the Titles that you are to give, the mutual Genuflections, the Turns you are to take sometimes to the Right and sometimes to the Left, the silent Civilities by which the Master of the House invites you to enter, the modest Refusal to enter first, the Salutation the Master of the House is to make to the Chair you are to sit in, for he must bow respectfully before it, and wipe off the Dust with the skirt of his garment,[35]

and by many other ridiculous dictates of fashion. Taking his idea from this source, Goldsmith in the letter from the Chinese lady, Yaoua, to her friend, Yaya, attempts to show the folly of such conduct. A second letter, supposedly written by an English lady, Belinda, to her confidante, Charlotte, describes the 'polite manners' of these ladies. It is introduced to show that the fashionable behavior of the English is no less absurd than that of the Chinese. In describing the Chinese call, Goldsmith, as might be expected, burlesques and renders even more shallow the mummery described by Du Halde. Further similarities, not mentioned here, may be found by a careful perusal of the *General History*[36] and of Letter XXXVII in the *Chinese Letters.*[37]

[35] *General History* 2. 187.
[36] *General History* 2. 184 ff.
[37] *Public Ledger*, March 23, 1760; *The Citizen of the World*, Letter XXXIX.

There are other examples of the use of Du Halde's *General History* as a source-book. Letter XLI of the *Chinese Letters*[38] was taken partly from this writer, and partly from Le Comte's *Memoirs and Observations*.[39] The purpose of this essay is to point out that the history of China is more replete with great actions than that of Europe. In order to do this, Goldsmith retold several surprising anecdotes of the virtue of three Chinese rulers, Tisiang, Ginsong, and Haitong. The first of these Goldsmith found in Le Comte; the second in Du Halde; while the third occurred in both writers. This last story, however, was undoubtedly taken from Du Halde, for he mentions, as does Goldsmith, that the name of the Emperor whom it concerned was Haitong, while Le Comte refers to him merely as 'one of the petty kings of Eastern Tartary'; more than this, Du Halde's account is somewhat more closely parallel to Goldsmith's than is Le Comte's.

Of the Emperor Gin tsong (the fourth emperor of the twentieth dynasty, called Yuen) Du Halde writes:

> Being inform'd that five Brethren were found guilty of a Crime, for which they were condemn'd to die, *Let one at least be pardoned,* says the Emperor, *that their unfortunate Parents may have somebody left to feed and comfort them.*[40]

This account Goldsmith alters, in the following way:

> When five brethren had set upon the great emperor Ginsong alone, with his sabre he slew four of them: he was struggling with the fifth, when his guards coming up were going to cut the conspirator into a thousand pieces. *No, no,* cried the emperor, with a calm placid countenance, *at least let one of the unfortunate family be suffered to live, that their poor aged parents may have some body left to feed and comfort them.*[41]

[38] *The Citizen of the World*, Letter XLII.
[39] See above, p. 121.
[40] *General History* I. 447.
[41] *Chinese Letters*, No. XLI.

The third anecdote, that relating to the emperor Haitong (the sixteenth and last emperor of the dynasty of Ming), is told by Du Halde in this way:

> Three Days after his Arrival [i. e. the arrival of the usurper Li, who advanced on the imperial city] the Gates were open'd, and he enter'd in a triumphant manner at the Head of 300,000 Men: The Emperor was shut up in his Palace, taken up with the foolish Superstitions of the Bonzes, not knowing what was doing in the City; but he could not remain long in this Ignorance, and when he found he was betray'd, would have gone out of the Palace with six hundred of his Guards, but they forsook him; being thus depriv'd of all Hopes, and chusing Death rather than to fall alive into the Hands of Rebels, he went into his Garden, and after he had wrote these Words on the Border of his Vest, *My subjects have basely abandon'd me; use me as you please, but Spare my People;* he kill'd his Daughter with the stroke of a Sabre, and hung himself upon a Tree.[42]

Goldsmith's account of the story is as follows:

> When Haitong, the last emperor of the house of Ming, saw himself besieged in his own city by the usurper, he was resolved to issue from his palace with six hundred of his guards, and give the enemy battle; but his guards forsook him. Being thus deprived of hopes, and chusing death rather than fall alive into the hands of a rebel, he retired to his garden, conducting an only child, his little daughter, in his hand. There in a private arbour unsheathing his sword, he stabbed the young innocent to the heart, and then dispatching himself, left the following words written with his blood on the border of his vest. *Forsaken by my subjects, abandoned by my friends, use my body as you will, but spare, O spare, my people.*[43]

The paragraph in Goldsmith's *Letter* directly following the above anecdotes praises the greatness of a country which,

---

[42] *General History* I. 478.
[43] *Chinese Letters*, Letter XLI.

'tho' at last conquered by the Tartars, still preserves its
antient laws and learning; and may more properly be said to
annex the dominions of Tartary to its empire, than to admit
a foreign conquerer.' Le Comte's account of the fusion of
the Chinese and Tartars is highly uncomplimentary to the
former;[44] so Goldsmith undoubtedly took his statements
from Du Halde, who tells us that in the reign of the first
emperor of the dynasty of Tsing, Chun Tchi 'shew'd himself so able in the Art of Government, that he soon gain'd
the Affection of his Subjects, and found the means to unite
the *Chinese* and *Tartars,* and make them as one Nation.'[45]

The above anecdotes serve as good examples to show
how Goldsmith used the ponderous, dull histories of China
to enliven his own essays with narrative interest.

In the *Chinese Letters,* Letter LXVII,[46] Goldsmith again
makes use of facts from the *General History*. In this
letter he satirizes the quack doctors, of whom there were
so many in the middle of the eighteenth century. Goldsmith's Chinese philosopher says that, in spite of the
supposed learning of Western physicians, 'I adhere to and
venerate the doctrines of old *Wang-shu-ho,*' and he adds
that 'In the very teeth of opposition I will maintain, *that
the heart is the son of the liver, which has the kidneys for
its mother, and the stomach for its wife.*' Goldsmith
acknowledges in a note to his essay that the remark is
taken from Du Halde.[47] It occurs in a Chinese book on
medicine, translated and included by Du Halde in his
history, entitled *The Secret of the Pulse,* a work attributed
to *Ouang tchou ho,*[48] where it appears in the following

[44] *Memoirs and Observations,* pp. 20-1.
[45] *General History* 2. 6.
[46] *The Citizen of the World,* Letter LXVIII.
[47] The footnote reads: 'See Du Halde, vol. II, fol. p. 185.'
Chinese Letters, Letter LXVII.
[48] *General History* 3. 413.

form: 'In the Spring-Season to have the Pulse of the Lungs is mortal; for the Pulse of the Heart is set aside, and the Heart is Son of the Liver, which has the Kidneys for its Mother, and the Stomach for its Wife.[49]

The next contribution of Du Halde to Goldsmith is found in *Public Ledger,* Letter LXXVI.[50] This essay deals with the cleverness of the shopkeepers as salesmen. Very often Goldsmith begins his essays with Oriental references and allusions, or with comparisons of England and China, and then falls into direct satire of his own nation. This is the case in this essay, which he opens with the following statement:

> The Shops of London are as well furnished as those of Pekin. Those of London have a picture hung at their door, informing the passengers what they have to sell, as those at Pekin have a board to assure the buyer that they have no intentions to cheat him.[51]

Knowledge of this detailed kind was acquired in Du Halde's and Le Comte's works. Du Halde's description of these sign boards is as follows:[52]

> *There are Shops adorned with China Ware, Silks, and Japan'd Goods; before the Door of every Shop there is placed a Pedestal, upon this is fix'd a Board seven or eight Foot high, either painted or gilt; upon this Board are wrote three large Characters, which the Tradesman chuses for the Sign of his Shop, to distinguish it from all others: There is sometimes inscribed on it two or three Sorts of Goods which are sold in the Shop, and at the Bottom the Trader's Name, with these words,* Pou hou, *that is to say, that he will not cheat you.*

[49] *General History* 3. 370.
[50] *The Citizen of the World,* Letter LXXVII.
[51] *Chinese Letters,* Letter LXXVI.
[52] *General History* 1. 108.

This is a good example of the way Goldsmith's books of reference served—to give Oriental atmosphere to his composition.

In the *Chinese Letters,* Letter LXXXII[53] contains a passage which Goldsmith insinuates was taken directly from a modern philosopher of China. He makes the insinuation in a note, which reads: 'A translation of this passage may also be seen in Du Halde.' Comparison of the *General History* with Goldsmith's essay proves conclusively that Goldsmith took the passage directly from Du Halde, and not from the original writing of 'the modern philosopher.' Du Halde quotes in his work a translation of this philosopher, under the heading, 'A Translation of a Chinese Author.' He nowhere mentions the author by name, but alludes to him in the *General History* as 'a modern Chinese philosopher.'[54] For that reason Goldsmith also designates the author in that way.

The essay under discussion opens with a brief introductory paragraph, in which Lien Chi Altangi admonishes his son, Hingpo, to sacrifice a few of the pleasures of the present, in order that he might enjoy greater happiness in the future. Then Lien Chi, instead of continuing the subject himself, lays before his son the precepts of 'the modern philosopher.' The portion of the essay which follows the introductory paragraph is a very loose paraphrase of different parts of Du Halde's *General History.* The rendering is so free, and the original so scattered and so long, that quotation here would not be practicable. The various general ideas on the value of reading, the education of children, etc., in Goldsmith's succeeding paragraphs, may be found by consulting the *General History.*[55] What Goldsmith says about romances, while undoubtedly his own

---

[53] *The Citizen of the World,* Letter LXXXIII.
[54] *General History* 3. 310.
[55] *General History* 3. 113, 353, 355 ff.

opinion[56] of that type of literature, is supported, as he says it is, by the reflections of Du Halde, who, referring to Chinese romances, writes:

> These Histories are not unlike our Romances which have been so much in fashion in these later Ages; but with this difference that our Romances are generally nothing but Love-adventures, or ingenious Fictions proper to divert the Reader, but at the same time that they divert so greatly captivate the Passions that they become very dangerous; especially to young Persons.[57]

Discussing the same topic, and still quoting 'the modern philosopher,' Goldsmith says:

> It was a saying of the ancients, that a man never opens a book without reaping some advantage by it.[58] I say with them, that every book can serve to make us more expert except romances, and these are no better than instruments of debauchery. They are dangerous fictions, where love is the ruling passion.[59]

Although Goldsmith quotes the entire essay as being the reflections of a modern philosopher of China, he is taking great liberties in doing so; for, while the general ideas are all to be found in Du Halde, the paraphrase is so free as to make the reflections appear Goldsmith's own.

Part of one of the *Chinese Letters,* Letter LXXXVII,[60] in which Lien Chi Altangi consoles his son with philosophy, finds its source in two books. Goldsmith states in a footnote to the essay: 'This letter is a rhapsody from The maxims of the philosopher Mé. Vide Lett. curieuses &

---

[56] Cf. *The Citizen of the World* 3. 285, and elsewhere.

[57] *General History* 3. 113.

[58] Cf. Percy's edition of Wilkinson's translation of *Hau Kiou Chooan* 3. 188: 'A man never opens a book without reaping some advantage from it.'

[59] *Chinese Letters,* Letter LXXXII.

[60] *The Citizen of the World,* Letter XCV.

édifiantes. Vide etiam Du Halde, vol. II, p. 98.' The sentiments of the first two paragraphs of Goldsmith's writing are taken from the *Lettres Curieuses et Edifiantes;* those of the last two paragraphs come from the *General History* of Du Halde. Lien Chi's injunction to Hingpo, that one must accept the circumstances of life as they come, has its source in these words of Yen, quoted in the *General History:*[61]

> This is the Moral of that ancient Fable: I saw a Gentleman riding before me on a fine Horse, whilst I was mounted upon an Ass; Ah! said I to myself, how different is my Condition from his! But, upon turning about my Head, I saw a good-looking Countryman driving a heavy Wheelbarrow before him; O then! said I, if I am not equal to him who goes before me, at least I am superior to him who follows me.

Lien Chi Altangi's advice to his son to be contented with his lot, however painful, is given by relating the same anecdote in this way:[62]

> But though I see you incapable of penetrating into grand principles, attend at least to a simile adapted to your apprehension. I am mounted upon a wretched ass. I see another man before me upon a sprightly horse at which I find some uneasiness. I look behind me and see numbers on foot stooping under heavy burdens, let me learn to pity their estate and thank heaven for my own.

The paragraph directly following this (it is the last paragraph of Goldsmith's letter), which contains a second anecdote, is likewise taken from Du Halde, from a quotation of his of a dialogue between the philosopher Lao-tse and his disciples. It is related by Tchin vou kouie, a modern

[61] *General History* 4. 64.
[62] *Chinese Letters,* Letter LXXXVII.

Chinese philosopher, who discusses religion and other matters with a crowd of young men, adherents of the sect of Fo. The text found in Du Halde reads:[63]

> I'll cite but one Place from the Instructions he [Lao tse] gave his Disciples: *Consider my Tongue,* said he to them, *does not it subsist while it remains soft and flexible? In the contrary, is not that which destroys our Teeth their own Hardness?"*

The version of this anecdote in the *Chinese Letters* reads:[64]

> You ask me a question cries the old man, let me answer by asking another, which is most durable a hard thing, or a soft thing, that which resists or that which make no resistance? *An hard thing to be sure,* replied the Mandarine. There you are wrong returned *Shingfu;* I am now forescore years old; and if you look in my mouth you'll find that I have lost all my teeth, but not a bit of my tongue.

The story of the griefs of Shingfu, to which the above anecdote enforces the moral, is closely parallel to the sorrows of Lien Chi himself; by citing it, Hingpo's father aimed to console his son for his own loss. This part of the story, as it is not found in Du Halde, and as it is only a slight variant of the Chinese wanderer's own experiences, was undoubtedly invented by Goldsmith in order to carry on the narrative interest of the frame-tale in the *Chinese Letters.*

The last time that Goldsmith drew materially from the *General History* was in Letter XCVII[65] of the *Public Ledger,* December 29, 1760. In this essay the Eastern philosopher explains to Beau Tibbs the Chinese attitude

---

[63] *General History* 3. 264.
[64] *Chinese Letters,* Letter LXXXVII.
[65] *The Citizen of the World,* Letter XCIX.

towards women.   That portion of the essay which deals with the ceremonies of the wedding night is taken from Du Halde. It is acknowledged by Goldsmith, in his pretended capacity as editor of the *Chinese Letters,* to have a parallel in that source.[66]   The portion referred to reads :[67]

> When the Ceremony is ended it is the Custom, in well-bred Families, for the young Bride to withdraw into her Apartment, and not to have any farther Concern with the rest of the Family, with her Brothers-in-law, nor even with her Husband's Father; and yet there has been introduced, even almost in our Days, among the Vulgar a detestable Custom, which I defy any one to find in our ancient Books, and which is only fit for Barbarians brought up and educated in a Desart: They delay her withdrawal into an Apartment for three Days, and these are called the *Three Days of Freedom;* and during this time what Extravagancies do not they allow to be put in practice?   The Wife is placed on the Nuptial-Bed; they flock round her, and perform a hundred Monkey-Tricks; one takes off her Shoes in a jesting manner, and hides them in her Sleeves; another lifts up the Veil which covers her Face; a third takes her Head between his Hands, smells her Hair, and cries, What an admirable Scent is here! Some counterfeit Madmen, and endeavour to raise a Laugh by Grimaces and indecent Buffooneries, at the same time drinking heavy Draughts; and this they call Merriment and Diversion.

Goldsmith copies his source rather closely in the following words :[68]

> Another ceremony, said I, resuming the conversation, in favour of the sex amongst us, is the bride's being allowed after marriage, *her three days of free-*

---

[66] *Chinese Letters,* No. XCVII, note (4): 'Vide Du Halde, Vol. II. Folio, p. 45.'

[67] *General History* 3. 341.

[68] *Chinese Letters,* Letter XCVII.

dom. During this interval a thousand extravagancies are practiced by either sex. The lady is placed upon the nuptial bed, and numberless monkey tricks are played round to divert her. One gentleman smells her perfumed handkerchief, another attempts to untie her garters,[69] a third pulls off her shoe to play hunt the slipper, another pretends to be an ideot, and endeavours to raise a laugh by grimacing; in the mean time the glass goes briskly about, till ladies, gentlemen, wife, husband, and all are mixed together in one inundation of arrack punch.

Le Comte and Du Halde furnished most of Goldsmith's Oriental erudition. The numerous details which are placed in an appendix furnish further information concerning the extent to which he was indebted to these two authors.

3. BYROM, JOHN. *Tom the Porter,* 1746.

A portion of Goldsmith's Letter in the *Public Ledger* of Jan. 31, 1760[70] is in substance reproduced from a poem of John Byrom's, entitled *Tom the Porter.*[71] This poem appeared first in the *Chester Courant* of Tuesday, Nov. 25, 1746, and was reprinted in *Manchester Vindicated.* It did not appear under Byrom's name until his poems were collected and edited in 1773; this was thirteen years after the appearance of Goldsmith's *Chinese Letters;* so Goldsmith apparently read it in either of the places first mentioned, where it was printed without being acknowledged by the author.

[69] Goldsmith introduces the old English custom of untying the bride's garters into his account of Chinese nuptial ceremonies.

[70] This letter is unnumbered in the *Public Ledger,* but is the fourth of the *Chinese Letters* in that periodical. In *The Citizen of the World,* the letter is numbered IV.

[71] The parallel between *Tom the Porter* and the *Chinese Letters,* Letter IV, has been noted by A. W. Ward. See *The Poems of John Byrom,* ed. Ward, 30. 297. Gibbs also points out the similarity of the two pieces (*Works* 3. 22, note 1).

The topic under discussion in Goldsmith's essay is English liberty. Sentiments about this subject, the author says, are echoed by all classes of society; for in Britain every man pretends to be a politician. Goldsmith illustrates how universally the problems of government are discussed, by recounting a conversation held before the gates of a prison. The dialogue which Goldsmith gives finds its source in the following verses by Byrom:

As *Tom* the Porter went up *Ludgate-Hill,*
A swingeing Show'r oblig'd him to stand still.
So, in the Right-hand Passage thro' the Gate
He pitch'd his Burden down, just by the Grate,
From whence the doleful Accent sounds away:
'Pity—the Poor—and Hungry—Debtors—pray.'

To the same Garrison from *Paul's* Church-yard
An half-drown'd Soldier ran to mount the Guard.
Now *Tom*, it seems, the *Ludgateer,* and he
Were old Acquaintance, formerly, all three;
And as the Coast was clear, by cloudy Weather,
They quickly fell into Discourse together.

'Twas in *December*, when the *Highland Clans*
Had got to *Derbyshire* from *Preston Pans,*
And struck all *London* with a general Panic;—
But mark the Force of Principles *Britannic!*

The Soldier told 'em fresh the City News,
Just piping hot from *Stockjobbers* and *Jews:*
Of *French* Fleets landing, and of *Dutch* Neutrality;
Of Jealousies at Court amongst the Quality;
Of *Swarston* Bridge, that never was pull'd down;
Of all the Rebels in full March to Town;
And of a hundred Things besides, that made
Lord May'r himself and Aldermen afraid,—
Painting with many an Oath the case in View;
And ask'd the Porter what he thought to do?

'Do?' says he, gravely; 'what I did before;
What I have done these thirty Years, and more:

Carry, as I am like to do, my Pack
Glad to maintain my Belly by my Back.
If that but hold, I care not, for my Part,
Come as come will, 't shall never break my Heart.
I don't see Folks that fight about their Thrones.
Mind either Soldiers' Flesh, or Porters' Bones.
Whoe'er gets better, when the Battle's fought,
Thy Pay nor mine will be advanc'd a Groat.
But, to the Purpose! Now we are met here,
Ill join, if t'will, for one full Mug of Beer.'

The Soldier, touch'd a little with Surprise
To see his Friend's Indifference, replies:
'What you say, *Tom*, I own, is very good,
But—OUR RELIGION!' and he d—n'd his Blood—

'What will become of OUR RELIGION? — 'True!'
Says the Jail-Bird— 'and of OUR FREEDOM too?
If the PRETENDER,' rapt he out, 'comes on,
OUR LIBERTIES AND PROPERTIES are gone!'

And so the Soldier and the Pris'ner join'd
To work up *Tom* into a better Mind.
He staring dumb, with Wonder struck and Pity.
Took up his Load and trudg'd into the City.

Goldsmith took the substance of the above verses for the topic of his essay, and to part of them wrote this prose paraphrase:[72]

> A few days ago as I was passing by one of their prisons, I could not avoid stopping, in order to listen to a dialogue which I thought might afford me some entertainment. The conversation was carried on between a debtor through the gate of his prison, a porter and a soldier at the window. The subject was a threatened invasion from France, and all seemed extremely anxious to rescue their country from impending danger. 'For my part, cries the prisoner, the

[72] *Public Ledger*, January 31, 1760.

greatest of my apprehension is for my freedom; if the French should conquer, what would become of English liberty. My dear friends, liberty is the Englishman's prerogative; we must preserve that at the expence of our lives, of that the French shall never deprive us; it is not to be expected that men who are slaves themselves would preserve our freedom should they happen to conquer. Ay, slaves, cries the porter, they are all slaves, fit only to carry burthens every one of them. Before I would stoop to slavery, may this be my poison (and he held the goblet in his hand) may this be my poison—but I would sooner list for a soldier.'

The soldier taking the goblet from his friend, with much awe fervently cried out, not our liberties, but our religion would suffer by such a change: ay, our religion, my friends; for may the devil sink me into flames, (such was the solemnity of his adjuration) if the French should come over, what would then become of our religion; so saying instead of a libation, he applied the goblet to his head, and confirm[73] his sentiments with every ceremony of sincere devotion.

It will be noticed that Goldsmith differs somewhat from his original; the persons engaged in the conversation, however, are the same as in Byrom, a poor debtor, a porter, and a soldier. The locality in each case is a prison, where the debtor is behind the bars, and the soldier and porter talk to him from without, through the grating.

4. JOHNSON, SAMUEL. *Rasselas*, 1759.

In writing the *Chinese Letters*, Letter XXXVI,[74] Goldsmith was undoubtedly influenced by Dr. Johnson's *Rasselas*.[75] The essay tells of the search for wisdom, and cites an allegory to prove its futility. Goldsmith asserts that this

[73] This is apparently a misprint for *confirmed*.
[74] *Public Ledger*, May 16, 1760; *The Citizen of the World*, Letter XXXVII.
[75] Gibbs also comments on this (*Works* 3. 139, footnote 1).

allegory is taken from the *Zendavesta* of Zoroaster;[76] it is, however, not to be found there, and is undoubtedly an invention of Goldsmith's, which bears resemblance to Dr. Johnson's novel. In his story, Goldsmith describes the early inhabitants of the world gathered in a peaceful valley, here living happily together. This valley is called the Valley of Ignorance, because of the simplicity of its inhabitants; and to their ignorance, the author claims, was due their happiness. At length an unfortunate youth, aspiring more than the rest, climbed the mountain side, and left the valley. This was the end of all his pleasures. The youth traveled in search of an unattainable goal, but soon wearied of his search, and desired to return to his Valley of Ignorance. It was too late, for, having plunged into the Ocean of Doubts, he could no longer return to his former state of innocence.

The Valley of Ignorance is copied from Johnson's Happy Valley, where the inhabitants lived in peace until one day, becoming too aspiring, they tunneled through the mountain, and went in search of greater happiness. After traveling about the world, they finally became aware of the futility of their search, and returned to their former secluded valley.

It is inconceivable that any one in 1760, reading Goldsmith's essay, should not notice its similarity to the universally popular *Rasselas,* which had appeared only the year before, in 1759. Goldsmith undoubtedly meant the parallel to be obvious. He used the allegory of the Valley of Ignorance to show the futility of searching for wisdom; Johnson used the allegory of the Happy Valley to show the futility of

---

[76] Miss Conant likewise comments on the resemblance of Goldsmith's paper to *Rasselas.* She says (*The Oriental Tale in England,* p. 196): 'The Valley of Ignorance, said by Goldsmith to be drawn from the *Zend-Avesta,* but resembling the Happy Valley of *Rasselas.'*

searching for happiness. Goldsmith, in copying Johnson's allegorical scheme, aimed to furnish pleasure by giving to an already familiar allegory a different application.

It was to this very understanding of the momentary interest of the public, to the timely choice of material, and to the popular mode of presenting the subject, that the *Chinese Letters* owed their success.

CHAPTER VII

Conclusion

The sources and literary relations of Goldsmith's *The Citizen of the World* are of importance, not because they show where the author found this or that fact, nor because they bring to light certain lost details, but because they clearly reveal his literary methods at a time when, as a young hack-writer, he was seeking fame; and also because they establish the character of the work which earned for its author a position of repute in the republic of letters.

The steps by which Goldsmith arrived at a determination to astonish the public with a series of Chinese pseudo-letters have been discussed at length in the preceding pages. Once having chosen a Chinese for a hero, having settled other details of his scheme, having read Marana and Montesquieu for models, and thus being well embarked upon the enterprise, he began to write about a land in the East of which he knew nothing, and in a manner which required considerable source-books. The contributions needed were derived from various originals, usually from the book most conveniently at hand. The works consulted were naturally of two types—pseudo-letters, and reference-books, chiefly Oriental. Of the former type, there were in English and French many examples prior to the use of that device in the *Chinese Letters*. Eight from this number served Goldsmith's periodical essays either for a general model, contributed concrete material to them, or did both. These are: Marana's *Espion Turc;* Addison's *Spectator,* No. 50; Montesquieu's *Lettres Persanes;* Lyttelton's *Letters from a Persian in England;* D'Argens' *Lettres Chinoises;* Voltaire's *Contradictions;* Voltaire's *Siècle de Louis XIV;* and Walpole's *Letter from Xo-Ho.* The second type, the reference-books which furnished Oriental and other material, are: Le Comte's *Nouveaux Mémoires;* Du Halde's *Histoire Générale;* Byrom's *Tom the Porter;* and Johnson's *Rasselas.*

It is more convenient to discuss this latter class, the reference-books, first. The reader must once more be reminded that Goldsmith was, when he began his composition of the *Chinese Letters,* almost entirely ignorant of the land about which he was to write. Therefore he took the two most available histories of China, namely those of Le Comte and Du Halde, and put them to systematic use. Chinese geographical names he found in the sections of these works which gave, in lists, descriptions of the provinces; Chinese history and historical anecdotes he found conveniently in chronological and abridged accounts of the Far-Eastern sovereigns; accounts of morality and moral sayings he found in the sections of those works which brought together the maxims of Eastern philosophers. Topics of this sort were easily located. In short, when the necessity arose for using material which was listed by the historians of China in chronological tables, Goldsmith merely looked up what he wanted, and used what he found. When his sources proved interesting, he did not hesitate to plagiarize the very words of the original version.

But these reference-works served Goldsmith to good purpose in another way. In the perusal of them, many useful details and even topics for essays lodged in his mind. Facts learned in this way were not accurately remembered, and thus Goldsmith's many curious slips, and his divergence in specific references from apparent sources, are easily accounted for. As it would have been difficult (except in the cases of tabulated subjects), on account of the bulkiness of his reference-books, and because of the fact that they contained no indexes, for Goldsmith to turn to the accounts he had read, and verify them, he wrote from memory. Moreover, it was not characteristic of Goldsmith to be scholarly. Further, it should be called to mind that as journalistic compositions are often hurriedly written, on account of the demands of the press, there is neither time nor opportunity to verify the references in them.

As an example of Goldsmith's use of his sources when he was merely writing from memory, Letter XXXVIII[1] in the *Public Ledger* is a good illustration. This paper deals with the ceremonies of a Chinese call. It shows that Goldsmith had been reading in Du Halde the account of Chinese ceremonies, in particular the one on visits. Being somewhat exasperated by the absurdities of the Chinese, and seeing the prevalence of similar artificialities and insincerity in English etiquette, Goldsmith was prompted to write a satirical essay on the subject. In his treatment of the topic, he did not follow Du Halde's version in detail; rather he wrote of the absurdities of his own invention, but yet in a hazy way followed his source. So Goldsmith not only received aid from Du Halde in matters of detail, but also had from that author inspiration for the composition of entire essays. In such cases, as a rule, he wrote after the details of the original version had been in part forgotten, and merely from the general impression which remained in his mind. This accounts for the lack of more accurate parallelisms than are found between Goldsmith's and Du Halde's accounts of the ceremonies of a Chinese visit, and in other places it also accounts for the haziness

---

[1] *The Citizen of the World*, Letter XXXIX.

of description in certain more specific references made by him; for example, of the animals mentioned in Letter VII,[2] the description of exotic beasts called the Shin Shin, the Gin Hiung, and the Boh, cited in one sentence. These are described by Du Halde in similar order on page 20 of his first volume. Of the strange animals Goldsmith says: 'Sure thou has been nurtured by the bill of the Shin Shin, or suck'd the breasts of the provident Gin Hiung. The melody of thy voice could rob the Choug Fou of her whelps, or inveigle the Boh Chou that lives amidst the water.' Du Halde's description of the animals follows.[3]

> That which they constantly affirm of the animal *Sin sin,* makes one think it a kind of an Ape . . . . There is another which they call *Gin-Hiung,* that is, a *Man-Bear,* which must be only understood of the extraordinary Bigness of that kind of Bears compared with Man . . . . But that which is related in their Books of the *Horse Tiger,* ought to be look'd upon as all fabulous. He does not differ, say they, in any thing from a Horse, but in his Scales wherewith he is covered, and by his Claws, which resemble a Tiger's; but more especially by his sanguinary Disposition, which makes him leave the Water in the Spring-Season, to devour both Man and Beast.

The reason for believing that Goldsmith learned of these fabulous animals in Du Halde is that they are not mentioned by writers about China, that they occur in similar grouping and similar order, are treated within limited space, and that certain details are sufficiently alike to identify them as the same animals, in Goldsmith and Du Halde. If Goldsmith had used this material as soon as he found it, he would not have referred to the bill of the Shin Shin, which was an ape; he would have been more accurate in his facts about the Gin Hiung, and he would have remembered something more about the Horse-Tiger, which he calls the Boh, than that it lived 'in the midst of the waters.' This is the kind of description which comes from confused memory. That one or two of the curious names, with some facts about the animals, should be remembered, is natural. That Goldsmith should try to find the place in Du Halde where he had read of the animals, and verify his description, was unnecessary for his purpose. His aim always was not to be a natural historian; it was merely to include some strange and surprising allusion to exotic matters, for the sake of interesting his readers by novelty, and convincing them of the Chinese authorship of the writer.

The *Chinese Letters* did not aim to instruct pedantically with facts; they attempted, when their purpose was not mere entertainment, to teach their readers to order their lives and opinions with sense and reason. Always with this in view, Goldsmith wrote in different ways, according to the necessity of the occasion. An example of each of his various ways of using his sources will suffice to show the methods employed by the young essayist.

The *Espion Turc* and the *Lettres Persanes* served Goldsmith merely as models; as very close models no doubt; and, if they contributed little concrete material to the *Chinese Letters,* their influence as inspiration was fully as great as, if not greater than, that of the works from which Goldsmith plagiarized. There cannot be the slightest doubt that Goldsmith, aided by Voltaire's criticism of Marana and Montesquieu in the 'Contradictions' and the *Siècle de Louis XIV,* was determined by that to compose a work after their manner, or that he learned in them all the elements of that device which places an Oriental in a strange land which he satirizes in a series of letters to his friends at home, which includes the answers of those friends, and which invents a frame-tale to hold together

the whole series, by giving it a thin narrative background
with plot-interest.[4] From Montesquieu, indeed, he may
have taken the name Zelis, and he undoubtedly had his
refutation of the critic's remarks on his style from that
source, and paraphrased at least one passage.[5] Various
topics of satire were perhaps suggested by Marana and
Montesquieu—topics which are subject to the satire of
any time and any nation, so that it would be absurd to
point out concrete examples which cannot with certainty be
proved. It is natural—very natural—that Goldsmith did
not use the *Espion Turc* or the *Lettres Persanes* for the
extraction of specific material; for these works were
known too widely to admit the concealment of plagiarized
material. That in itself is sufficient to explain Goldsmith's
attitude with regard to those works. On the other hand,
Lyttelton's *Persian Letters* and D'Argens' *Lettres Chinoises*
were sufficiently obscure to admit of closer and more
specific use by Goldsmith. Take, for example, a case in
which he drew material from them. Let us for the
moment speculate that, in instances where Goldsmith copied
his sources word for word, the following happened—
that on the day he wrote his letter for February 20, 1760,
he had dined and wined at the Grecian Coffee House, and
let his evening work-hours pass by in pleasant conversation; that, returning home, he remembered that his essay
for the *Public Ledger* for the morrow was still unwritten,
and that his observations furnished no suitable subject; that
Newbery was strict about having the papers; that his
pocket-book was empty; that he got a guinea for each
letter; that copying was easier than composing. Goldsmith slipped D'Argens' letters from the book-shelf, turned
over the pages, saw the heading 'Funeral Solemnities of
the Daurs,' smiled, and ran his fingers down the page.

[4] See above, p. 46 ff.
[5] See above, p. 48-50.

He copied the source almost word for word; time was pressing, and Goldsmith did not hesitate to take from the pages of another author his contribution to the *Public Ledger* of the day. Let us speculate that, when writing Letter IX in the *Chinese Letters,* the same thing happened. It is taken from D'Argens' Letter XXI.[6]

Goldsmith's method of using this material is clear. He did not read over the pages of D'Argens and write from memory; he read down the page with his finger on the text, as it were, and put down idea for idea, and often phrase for phrase, without changing the relative order of a single thought. The structure of D'Argens' essay he accepted as it stood. Goldsmith altered certain details to suit English rather than French conditions. He condensed. He perfected the style. Toward the end of the essay he shifted the emphasis of the satire, which in D'Argens was directed against adultery, to a ridicule of the loose habits of London fops. He concluded the essay with a burlesque list of rules of conduct for men of fashion, which is very similar to Beau Nash's 'Rules to be observed at Bath.' This latter list Goldsmith included entire in his *Memoirs* of that London dandy, which appeared less than two years later. The mere suggestion of the villainy of 'Men of Fashion' by D'Argens—for he does not develop the theme—started Goldsmith on a new track, and he amplified a subject the consideration of which rankled in his heart.

There are other cases in which Goldsmith has used his material differently. For example, to continue to draw illustrations from D'Argens, Goldsmith has taken Letter XVI of *The Citizen of the World* almost word for word from D'Argens' Letter XXXI; but he has changed the order of thoughts; he has altered the structure; and, from

[6] See texts, pp. 82-84.

a dull, disorderly essay, has made an entertaining and charming narrative. In the cases already mentioned, he wrote with his finger on the text of his source; in other cases he read through the material in his source, and re-wrote from memory, often substituting concrete examples of his own to illustrate general principles found in the pages of Marana, Montesquieu, or Lyttelton.

To illustrate the importance of this study of sources, it is convenient to return to the essay dealing with English morality. Great credit has been given to Goldsmith for being the originator of the idea that the English penal code was unjustly severe. His insight into the social conditions of the time has been praised. He has been quoted as the philosopher whose penetration into human nature enabled him to make such wise observations on the evils of the day, or as the humanitarian who instituted the beginning of social reform. Both Prior and Forster, who have written standard biographies of Goldsmith, include this essay in lists quoted for the purpose of showing that their author possessed critical insight above the other essayists of his time. When it is found that the idea was not original with Goldsmith, but was D'Argens' idea, the only conclusion to be drawn is that his originality is not so great as his editors and biographers have proclaimed. Numerous examples of this kind show that Goldsmith has been falsely estimated.

It must not be thought, however, that Goldsmith's rather extensive borrowings belittle his real genius. To discover these is rather to prove the opposite. 'Qui nullum fere scribendi genus non tetigit, nullum quod tetigit non ornavit.' The entangled and uninteresting details of Boyer reappeared without confusion on the page of Goldsmith; the obscure verbosity of Du Halde became exact and unconstrained prose. To make similar points, Goldsmith used only half the material required by the sources. The disorderly essays he pillaged for his Oriental erudition, transformed in *The Citizen of the World,* assumed perfect structure. His manner was in every case superior to the style of his predecessor. His humor enlivened everything he treated. For example, in George Lyttelton we read that a lady of distinction, being curious to talk with an Oriental, had a Persian brought to her apartment. On his entrance, the lady greeted him with great satisfaction, saying she had been curious to know a Mohammedan, who lived so far away. In describing the parallel circumstance Goldsmith makes his lady, as soon as the Oriental enters the room, shout out: 'So you are the gentleman who was born so far from home.'

In humor, Goldsmith surpassed the writers he imitated. The fact that many of the ideas he expressed were not original with him does not lessen his genius as a writer. No one ever justly called Goldsmith a deep thinker. No one ever justly said that he is not one of the foremost of English authors. No one can say that Goldsmith was a great scholar; yet no one can deny him wisdom. Like his Chinese philosopher, Goldsmith aimed to know the men of every country by knowing the human heart, and thus, by exposing the faults of the English nation, to teach it wisdom. 'On peut être bien sage sans être érudit.'

It is by these things that the character of *The Citizen of the World* is established. In the composition of the version which appeared in the *Public Ledger,* Goldsmith made his first great attempt to go beyond hack-writing, and produce something of permanent literary worth. He tried to avoid mere journalism. Only in part did he succeed in this ambition; for in a sense the *Chinese Letters* were hack-writing. By this term I mean composition which is forced hurriedly from the pen, and done under pressure, with drudgery. Many of the essays in *The Citizen of the World* show traces of that kind of writing. By journalistic writing I mean composition which is for one age, not for all time, writing which deals with subjects of passing interest, and results which are of transitory value. After the Beau Tibbs essays, the 'City Night-Piece,' and some other letters which as literary essays are unsurpassed in the English language, are subtracted, a vast residue of material remains which has lost its interest to-day, because the material was presented for the perusal of readers in the years 1760 and 1761. Its interest is lost, because Goldsmith's attempt was first and foremost for contemporary popularity; and, in a sense, its value is retained for the same reason. The interest in these examples is not so great to the *littérateur,* but to the historian it is paramount, for in the pages of the *Chinese Letters* he finds the most comprehensive account of the times when George II died, and his successor followed him to the throne.

For this contemporary interest, Goldsmith put forth his greatest efforts, using every device to make for popularity. His choice of China for Oriental background was to conform to the prevailing fad; but it must not be forgotten that Goldsmith was choosing that land which Voltaire praised, to do for English satire what Montesquieu had done for French. For contemporary appeal, Goldsmith chose the pseudo-letter device, for that was relatively new, and so of interest to the English, but he also chose that device because it offered an opportunity to write a classic example of that *genre* in the English language. For contemporary appeal, he wrote of the coronation procession of King George, of the hanging of Earl Ferrers with a silken rope, of the country cart-race, and of a hundred other things. For contemporary appeal, he used the familiar allegory of *Rasselas* with a new application—to please his audience with the old theme handled in a new way.

At first Goldsmith's hopes lay entirely in writing a great literary masterpiece; the manner under which he, as a journalist, was forced to write his papers, caused the change to an essentially journalistic appeal. With the publication of

The Citizen of the World, he made a new effort for literary effectiveness. He made elaborate changes in nearly every essay. He polished; he smoothed his writing; he inserted paragraphs; he omitted poorly written passages, and un-essentials; he gave structure to formless compositions. All this he did with great care, but it availed him little. The newspaper essays gave him reputation; *The Citizen of the World* did little to augment his fame. The reviews of this publication were unsatisfactory, and only mildly lauda-tory. By the time the second edition had appeared, the author of *The Citizen of the World* had realized the futility of further revision. The second edition of 1769 and the third edition of 1774 are practically reprints of the first edition. *The Citizen of the World* is a great work. Its greatness lies in its influence on the age in which it was written. It is an important work, and its value, on the whole, is to those who care to know the England of 1760. But, further than that, it contains some dozen essays which are literary masterpieces. It remains the greatest work of its kind in the annals of periodic literature in the latter half of the eighteenth century, while it is undisputably the classic example of the pseudo-letter in the English language.

TABLE OF DATES TO THE *CHINESE LETTERS*

[Thirty-three of Goldsmith's *Chinese Letters* have hitherto been undated. A complete list of the dates of the essays follows below. As the order of the letters was changed with the compilation of *The Citizen of the World,* a key to the numbering is subjoined. In column one, the corrected numbering of the letters in *The Citizen* edition is given; in column two is found the corresponding number of *The Public Ledger* edition; and in column three is placed the date on which the letter first appeared in the London newspaper.]

CITIZEN NUMBER	PUBLIC LEDGER NUMBER	PUBLIC LEDGER DATE
Preface	[none]	
I	unnumbered	Jan. 24, 1760
II	unnumbered	Jan. 24, 1760
III	unnumbered	Jan. 29, 1760
IV	unnumbered	Jan. 31, 1760
V	VI	Feb. 7, 1760
VI	IV	Feb. 1, 1760
VII	V	Feb. 4, 1760
VIII	VII	Feb. 9, 1760
IX	VIII	Feb. 12, 1760
X	IX	Feb. 14, 1760
XI	X	Feb. 18, 1760
XII	XI	Feb. 21, 1760
XIII	XII	Feb. 25, 1760
XIV	XIII	Feb. 28, 1760
XV	XIV	Mar. 5, 1760
XVI	XV	Mar. 11, 1760
XVII	XVI	Mar. 13, 1760
XVIII	XVII	Mar. 15, 1760
XIX	XVIII	Mar. 18, 1760
XX	XIX	Mar. 20, 1760
XXI	XX	Mar. 21, 1760
XXII	XXI	Mar. 24, 1760
XXIII	XXII	Mar. 25, 1760
XXIV	XXIII	Mar. 27, 1760
XXV	XXIV	Apr. 1, 1760
XXVI	XXV	Apr. 3, 1760
XXVII	XXVI	Apr. 9, 1760
XXVIII	XXVIII	Apr. 16, 1760
XXIX	XXVII	Apr. 14, 1760
XXX	XXXII	May 2, 1760
XXXI	XXIX	Apr. 18, 1760
XXXII	XXX	Apr. 22, 1760
XXXIII	XXXI	Apr. 25, 1760
XXXIV	XXXIII	May 6, 1760
XXXV	XXXIV	May 12, 1760
XXXVI	XXXV	May 14, 1760
XXXVII	XXXVI	May 16, 1760
XXXVIII	XXXVII	May 19, 1760
XXXIX	XXXVIII	May 23, 1760

CITIZEN NUMBER	PUBLIC LEDGER NUMBER	PUBLIC LEDGER DATE
XL	XXXIX	May 26, 1760
XLI	XL	May 28, 1760
XLII	XLI	May 30, 1760
XLIII	XLII	June 3, 1760
XLIV	XLIII	June 6, 1760
XLV	XLIV	June 9, 1760
XLVI	XLV	June 10, 1760
XLVII	XLVI	June 12, 1760
XLVIII	XLVII	June 17, 1760
XLIX	*XLVIII	June 18, 1760
L	XLVIII	June 19, 1760
LI	XLIX	June 23, 1760
LII	L	June 24, 1760
LIII	LI	June 30, 1760
LIV	LII	July 2, 1760
LV	LX	Aug. 1, 1760
LVI	LIII	July 8, 1760
LVII	LIV	July 9, 1760
LVIII	LV	July 18, 1760
LIX	LVI	July 21, 1760
LX	LVIII	July 24, 1760
LXI	LVII	July 23, 1760
LXII	LIX	July 28, 1760
LXIII	LXIV	Aug. 13, 1760
LXIV	LXII	Aug. 6, 1760
LXV	LXIII	Aug. 12, 1760
LXVI	LXV	Aug. 19, 1760
LXVII	LXVI	Aug. 22, 1760
LXVIII	LXVII	Aug. 25, 1760
LXIX	LXVIII	Aug. 29, 1760
LXX	LXIX	Sept. 1, 1760
LXXI	LXX	Sept. 2, 1760
LXXII	LXXI	Sept. 10, 1760
LXXIII	LXXII	Sept. 12, 1760
LXXIV	LXXIII	Sept. 15, 1760
LXXV	LXXIV	Sept. 17, 1760
LXXVI	LXXV	Sept. 19, 1760

* The letters of July 18 and July 19, 1760, were both numbered XLVIII in the *Public Ledger*.

Citizen Number	Public Ledger Number	Public Ledger Date
LXXVII	LXXVI	Sept. 22, 1760
LXXVIII	LXXVII	Sept. 26, 1760
LXXIX	LXXVIII	Sept. 30, 1760
LXXX	LXXIX	Oct. 3, 1760
LXXXI	LXXX	Oct. 6, 1760
LXXXII	LXXXI	Oct. 10, 1760
LXXXIII	LXXXII	Oct. 15, 1760
LXXXIV	LXXXIII	Oct. 17, 1760
LXXXV	LXXXIV	Oct. 21, 1760
LXXXVI	LXXXV	Oct. 24, 1760
LXXXVII	LXXXVIII	Oct. 31, 1760
LXXXVIII	XCI	Nov. 14, 1760
LXXXIX	XCIII	Nov. 21, 1760
XC	XCVI	Dec. 17, 1760
XCI	XCII	Nov. 17, 1760
XCII	XCV	Dec. 3, 1760
XCIII	XCIX	Jan. 7, 1761
XCIV	LXXXVI	Oct. 27, 1760
XCV	LXXXVII	Oct. 29, 1760
XCVI	LXXXIX	Nov. 5, 1760
XCVII	XC	Nov. 7, 1760
XCVIII	XCIV	Nov. 28, 1760
XCIX	XCVII	Dec. 29, 1760
C	XCVIII	Jan. 2, 1761
CI	C	[Jan. 5, 1761]*
CII	CI	Jan. 13, 1761
CIII	CII	[Jan. 18, 1761]*
CIV	CIII	Jan. 26, 1761
CV	CIV	Feb. 10, 1761
CVI	†CVI	Mar. 4, 1761
CVII	CV	Feb. 20, 1761
CVIII	†CVI	Feb. 27, 1761
CIX	CVIII	Mar. 18, 1761
CX	CXII	May 1, 1761

* Numbers CCCXII and CCCXX of the *Public Ledger* are missing from the British Museum file; these appeared on January 5 and January 18 of 1761, and undoubtedly contained letters CI and CII of the *Chinese Letters.*

† The letters of February 27 and March 4, 1761, were both numbered CVI in the *Public Ledger.*

CITIZEN NUMBER	PUBLIC LEDGER NUMBER	PUBLIC LEDGER DATE
CXI	CVII	Mar. 11, 1761
CXII	CIX	Apr. 3, 1761
CXIII	CX	Apr. 14, 1761
CXIV	CXI	Apr. 21, 1761
CXV	CXIII	May 8, 1761
CXVI	CXIV	May 13, 1761
CXVII	City Night Piece—not in *Public Ledger*.	
CXVIII	LXI	Aug. 5, 1760
CXVIX	Not in *Public Ledger*.	
CXX	CXV	July 8, 1761
CXXI	Not in *Public Ledger*.	
CXXII	Not in *Public Ledger*.	
CXXIII	CXVI	Aug. 14, 1761

KEY TO THE CORRESPONDENCE IN NUMBERING BETWEEN THE *CHINESE LETTERS* AND VARIOUS EDITIONS OF *THE CITIZEN OF THE WORLD*.

[Owing to several errors in numbering the essays of the *Chinese Letters*, and those of the early editions of *The Citizen of the World*, the numbers of the same essays in the different essays do not correspond. A further lack of correspondence in numbering is brought about by the addition of several letters to *The Citizen of the World* edition, which did not appear in the *Public Ledger*. In order to make possible reference from one edition to another, the following table is subjoined.

The errors in numbering are as follows:

The *Chinese Letters* (in the *Public Ledger*). Each of the following numbers used for two consecutive letters: 47 and 106. *The Citizen of the World*, (First and Third Editions): Each of the following numbers is used for two consecutive letters: 25, 49, 57, 116.]

Citizen of the World Corrected numbering as given in modern editions.	Citizen of the World Numbering of the First and Third editions.	Chinese Letters Numbering of *Public Ledger* edition.
		. . . .
Preface	Preface	
I	I	unnumbered
II	II	unnumbered
III	III	unnumbered
IV	IV	unnumbered
V	V	VI
VI	VI	IV
VII	VII	V
VIII	VIII	VII
IX	IX	VIII
X	X	IX
XI	XI	X
XII	XII	XI
XIII	XIII	XII
XIV	XIV	XIII
XV	XV	XIV
XVI	XVI	XV
XVII	XVII	XVI
XVIII	XVIII	XVII
XIX	XIX	XVIII
XX	XX	XIX
XXI	XXI	XX
XXII	XXII	XXI
XXIV	XXIV	XXIII
XXV	XXV	XXIV
XXVI	XXV	XXV
XXVII	XXVI	XXVI
XXVIII	XXVII	XXVIII
XXIX	XXVIII	XXVII
XXX	XXIX	XXXII
XXXI	XXX	XXIX
XXXII	XXXI	XXX
XXXIII	XXXII	XXXI
XXXIV	XXXIII	XXXIII
XXXV	XXXIV	XXXIV
XXXVI	XXXV	XXXV
XXXVII	XXXVI	XXXVI
XXXVIII	XXXVII	XXXVII

CITIZEN OF THE WORLD	CITIZEN OF THE WORLD	CHINESE LETTERS
Corrected numbering as given in modern editions.	Numbering of the First and Third editions.	Numbering of *Public Ledger* editions.
XXXIX	XXXVIII	XXXVIII
XL	XXXIX	XXXIX
XLI	XL	XL
XLII	XLI	XLI
XLIII	XLII	XLII
LXIV	XLIII	XLIII
XLV	XLIV	XLIV
XLVI	XLV	XLV
XLVII	XLVI	XLVI
XYVIII	XLVII	XLVII
XLIX	XLVIII	XLVIII
L	XLIX	XLVIII
LI	XLIX	XLIX
LII	L	L
LIII	LI	LI
LIV	LII	LII
LV	LIII	LX
LVI	LIV	LIII
LVII	LV	LIV
LVIII	LVI	LV
LIX	LVII	LVI
LX	LVII	LVIII
LXI	LVIII	LVII
LXII	LIX	LIX
LXIII	LX	LXIV
LXIV	LXI	LXII
LXV	LXII	LXIII
LXVI	LXIII	LXV
LXVII	LXIV	LXVI
LXVIII	LXV	LXVII
LXIX	LXVI	LXVIII
LXX	LXVII	LXIX
LXXI	LXVIII	LXX
LXXII	LXIX	LXXI
LXXIII	LXX	LXXII
LXXIV	LXXI	LXXIII
LXXV	LXXII	LXXIV
LXXVI	LXXIII	LXXV

Citizen of the World Corrected numbering as given in modern editions.	Citizen of the World Numbering of the First and Third editions.	Chinese Letters Numbering of *Public Ledger* editions.
LXXVII	LXXIV	LXXVI
LXXVIII	LXXV	LXXVII
LXXIX	LXXVI	LXXVIII
LXXX	LXXVII	LXXIX
LXXXI	LXXVIII	LXXX
LXXXII	LXXIX	LXXXI
LXXXIII	LXXX	LXXXII
LXXXIV	LXXXI	LXXXIII
LXXXV	LXXXII	LXXXIV
LXXXVI	LXXXIII	LXXXV
LXXXVII	LXXXIV	LXXXVIII
LXXXVIII	LXXXV	XCI
LXXXIX	LXXXVI	XCIII
XC	LXXXVII	XCVI
XCI	LXXXVIII	XCII
XCII	LXXXIX	XCV
XCIII	XC	XCIX
XCIV	XCI	LXXXVI
XCV	XCII	LXXXVII
XCVI	XCIII	LXXXIX
XCVII	XCIV	XC
XCVIII	XCV	XCIV
XCIX	XCVI	XCVII
C	XCVII	XCVIII
CI	XCVIII	C
CII	XCIX	CI
CIII	C	CII
CIV	CI	CIII
CV	CII	CIV
CVI	CIII	CVI
CVII	CIV	CV
CVIII	CV	CVI
CIX	CVI	CVIII
CX	CVII	CXII
CXI	CVIII	CVII
CXII	CIX	CIX
CXIII	CX	CX
CXIV	CXI	CXI

CITIZEN OF THE WORLD	CITIZEN OF THE WORLD	CHINESE LETTERS
Corrected numbering as given in modern editions.	Numbering of the First and Third editions.	Numbering of *Public Ledger* editions.
CXV	CXII	CXIII
CXVI	CXIII	CXIV
CXVII	CXIV	Not in *Public Ledger*. Appeared in the *Bee*, Oct. 27, 1759.
CXVIII	CXV	LXI
CXIX	CXVI	Not in *Public Ledger*. Appeared in the *British Magazine*.
CXXX	CXVI	CXV
CXXI	CXVII	Not in *Public Ledger*. Written for *The Citizen of the World*.
CXXII	CXXIII	Not in *Public Ledger*. Written for *The Citizen of the World*.
CXXIII	CXIX	CXVI

A. Further partial list of books containing the foreign-observer device, or otherwise suggesting *The Citizen of the World*

(This list includes only English originals, and English translations of foreign works.)

1. 1647. G. U., alias PHILOPARTHASS ESDRASS. *Grand Plato's Progress through Great Britain and Ireland.*

This poem suggests *The Citizen of the World* device. The sub-title explains that it is Grand Plato's 'Diarie, or exact Journale of his Observations during the time of his walking to and fro in the said Kingdoms. Found on Dunsmore Heath, and translated out of Infernall Characters into English Verse.'

2. 1665. BOYLE, ROBERT. *Occasional Reflections Upon Several Subjects. Whereto is Premised a Discourse about such kind of Thoughts.*[1]

To Robert Boyle must be given the credit of formulating, at the early date of about 1665, a device which is in essence the device of the latter successful *Espion Turc, Lettres Persanes,* and *The Citizen of the World;* for in his *Occasional Reflections* he used intelligent but imaginary foreigners as the mouthpieces of veiled satire, which he brought to bear on the foibles of his native land. The foreigners are named Eugenius and Generio; they are travelers and gentlemen; and their criticism is to be found in the dialogues which are from time to time interspersed through the volume. These are of moral, philosophical, and satirical trend. Although the device used contains only a part of the more elaborate scheme of the pseudo-letter *genre,* the *Occasional Reflections* should be given credit for being an early work which formulates its essential underlying idea.

3. 1666. DUCHESS OF NEWCASTLE. *The Blazing World.*

The Citizen of the World device is suggested, in that the empress of the blazing world visits England, and comments on what she sees.

4. 1691; 1693. GILDON, CHARLES. *The Post-Boy Robb'd of his Mail or, the Pacquet Broke Open. Consisting of Letters of Love and Gallantry, and all Miscellaneous Subjects: In which are discover'd the Vertues, Vices, Follies, Humor and Intrigues of Mankind.*[2]

Charles Gildon's *Post-Boy Robb'd of his Mail* was built

---

[1] *The Works of the Honorable Robert Boyle,* London, 1772, 2. 323-461.
[2] The first edition of *The Post-Boy Robb'd of his Mail,* 1691, was in one volume; a second volume appeared in 1693. The second edition, which included both volumes, appeared in 1706.

upon a new and effective plan for presenting satirical material. The author aims to reveal widespread English opinion by printing the contents of all the letters in a public mail-bag. Certain gentlemen rob the post-boy and retire to a nearby coffee-house, where they indulge in a discussion of the sentiments expressed in the stolen letters; needless to say, they are of Gildon's composition.

Volume I of *The Post-Boy Robb'd of his Mail* resembles the *Chinese Letters* only in being a satire of London conditions in a series of letters of feigned authorship. Volume II, however, adds another element of the *Chinese Letters* device by introducing critical correspondence from an Oriental. A strong hint is given that the Asiatic was a Chinese spy in Europe. Undoubtedly Gildon copied the device from Marana's *Turkish Spy*.

The Asiatic letters are twelve in number; they are addressed to 'Sir John R—bts, *at his house near Bedford* .... *from the wandering* Honan, to the *dearest of his friends.*'[3] They are written originally in English, and in this respect differ from the pseudo-letters of Marana, Montesquieu, and Goldsmith, which purport to be translations. Gildon gives only one side of the correspondence—the letters from Honan to his friend. They are philosophical and moral, not satirical. Sent from various parts of Europe, Asia, and Africa, they deal largely with expositions of the religions found in the various states through which Honan traveled. From these papers Goldsmith drew no concrete facts nor traceable ideas.[4]

---

[3] In *The Post-Boy Robb'd of his Mail,* ed. 1706, pp. 230-291.
[4] See *Journal of English and Germanic Philology,* Vol. 8, No. 2, April, 1909, review of Conant's *Oriental Tale in England,* by C. N. Greenough.

5. 1698. [KING, WILLIAM] *A Journey to London.*[5]

The title-page of *A Journey to London* states that this tract was 'Written Originally in French, by Monsieur Sorbière, and Newly Translated into English.' The true author, however, is William King. By giving out a pretended anonymous translation, he makes Samuel Sorbière appear to burlesque one of his own accounts of England.[6] Of this piece, which had been published in 1664, Voltaire wrote:

> I would not imitate the late M. Sorbière, who having stayed three months in England, without knowing anything either of its manners or its language, thought fit to print a relation which proved but a dull scurrilous satire upon a nation he knew nothing of.

Thus the use of the imaginary observer occurs in *A Journey to London,* from the device used for burlesque of writings which give feigned accounts of England, and are filled with errors, rather than from intent to employ a foreigner to satirize English manners, a result which it also in some degree achieves.

6. 1698. WARD, EDWARD. *The London Spy.*

Ned Ward's *London Spy,* originally published in monthly folio parts, beginning in November, 1698, was 'printed compleat in eighteen parts,' in 1703. It is a work which, like Du Fresny's *Amusemens Sérieux et Comiques,* aimed at exposing the vices and follies of city life. The name was probably drawn from the familiar *Turkish Spy* of Marana. Ward tells the design of his book in the first pages: A young

---

[5] Reprinted in *A Miscellany of the Wits,* edited by K. N. Colvile, M.A.

[6] The occasion of King's burlesque was the publication of *A Journey to Paris,* by one Dr. Martin Lister. See *A Miscellany of Wits,* p. xvii.

man, tired of his confinement in the country and of his much reading, comes to London, and spies upon the corruption of the city. His observations are confined largely to the sordidness of gambling, whoring, pimping, and the evils of Eastcheap.

The observations are not those of a foreigner, but of a native; the work is not written in letter-form; so its only resemblance to the pseudo-letter *genre* is in the device of having a critic of English manners and morals travel through the city, and satirize its foibles.

7. 1699. Du Fresny, Charles Rivière. *Amusemens Sérieux et Comiques.*[7]

Du Fresny's *Amusemens Sérieux et Comiques* followed shortly upon Marana's *Espion Turc* in the use of the device which utilized a foreigner to criticize conditions at home. For this purpose the author assumed the guise of a Siamese instead of a Turkish observer, and satirized the more vulgar sides of Parisian life. He discussed such topics as gaming, whoring, the theatre, the promenades, marriage, gallantry, and Paris coffee-houses. The satire is mild, general, and on the whole lacks acuteness, as well as originality of point of view. Du Fresny's book differs from the pseudo-letter *genre* by presenting the material in a series of satirical sketches called 'Amusemens,' instead of in the usual form of correspondence between the traveling foreigner and his friends at home.

We are aware that Goldsmith knew Du Fresny's work through the often cited selection from Voltaire, which praised the use of the satiric method. The portion of the *Amusemens Sérieux et Comiques* which most closely resembles Goldsmith's is *Amusemen III, Paris;* but even this

---

[7] The first edition of the *Amusemens Sérieux et Comiques* appeared in 1699, at Paris. The original French text, with parallel columns of an English translation, was printed in 1719.

section has no resemblance except in the similar topic of city life. The French author deals with sordid conditions, while Goldsmith treats of more genteel manners. In the entire book there is no evidence that Goldsmith used Du Fresny's work as a source-book.

8. 1700 BROWN, THOMAS. *Amusements Serious and Comical Calculated for the Meridian of London, separately published in 1700; and also in the Works of Thomas Brown, in three volumes, with a character of the Author by James Drake, M.D. 1707-1708.*

Thomas Brown's *Amusements Serious and Comical Calculated for the Meridian of London* is a development of the pseudo-letter *genre* which comes directly from Du Fresny.[8] It is, in fact, partly a verbal translation, though unacknowledged, and partly a paraphrase of *Les Amusemens Sérieux et Comiques;* but, to the more general plan of Du Fresny, Brown adds concrete satire of the lower side of London life, quite similar to that of Ned Ward and Daniel Defoe.

Amusement III, called *London,* in Brown's Book, is based on Du Fresny's *Amusemen* III, which concerns Paris. In this *Amusement* is found the use of *The Citizen of the World* device. Here it is stated that an Indian will be given an opportunity to see and criticize London. It is not surprising that the Indian visitor went to see the same sights as did Lien Chi Altangi; for what traveler would not go to the theatres, to Hyde Park—to the Abbey, Nor is it surprising that both critics should satirize fops, beaux, coquettes, quacks, plays, gambling. There is nothing in Brown's brutal satire specifically comparable to Goldsmith's. But it will be seen that the general scheme of the work, the Indian's comparison of London manners with his native conditions, the use of Oriental material as a vehicle of satire, is closely parallel to *The Citizen of the World.*

[8] See above, pp. 136-7.

9. 1704. SWIFT, JONATHAN.

The following advertisement is found opposite the title-
page of the first edition of Swift's *Tale of a Tub,* 1704, in
a list of 'Treatises writ by the same Author . . . which will
be speedily published'. It reads: 'A Voyage into England,
by a Person of Quality in Terra Australia incognita, translated from the Original.' Needless to say, Swift did not
publish this supposed translation. It was the project which
he mentioned in his letter to Stella, April 28, 1711:

> *The Spectator* is written by Steele, with Addison's
> help; 't is often very pretty. Yesterday it was made of
> a noble hint I gave him long ago for his Tatlers, about
> an Indian supposed to write his travels into England.[9]
> I repent he ever did it. I intended to have written a
> book on that subject. I believe he has spent it all in
> one paper, and all the under hints are mine too.[10]

As the paper is Addison's, not Steele's, the latter probably
communicated the project to his friend.

Prior suggests that Swift's advertisement may have been
of assistance to Goldsmith. In discussing *The Citizen of
the World* he says:[11]

> Swift had formed some such design, though not
> wholly the same, from the greater rudeness of the people
> who were introduced as giving the fruits of their obser-
> vation, in making the Indian chiefs who were in London
> during the reign of Queen Anne tell the story of their
> travels; a project which by communicating to Steele,
> the latter marred by a paper or two in the 'Tatler' and
> 'Spectator'.

[9] The paper on 'The Four Indian Kings' is here alluded to. It is
Spectator, No. 50, which appeared April 27, 1711. It should be noticed
that on April 28 Swift referred to *The Spectator* of 'yesterday.'
This definitely establishes the letter on 'The Four Indian Kings' as
the one Swift refers to, for it appeared on April 27.

[10] *Letters to Stella,* dated April 28, 1711. For further discussion,
see above pp. 43-5.

[11] *Life* I. 358-9.

If Goldsmith was aware of Swift's hint to Steele, he must undoubtedly have been pleased to have sanction for his project of the *Chinese Letters,* from an author so highly esteemed as Swift.[12]

10. 1705. DEFOE, DANIEL. *The Consolidator: or Memoirs of Sundry Transactions from the World in the Moon, Translated from the Lunar Language. By the Author of the True-Born Englishman, London, . . .* 1705.

Defoe's *Consolidator* is a prose satire, in which a Chinese, the supposed author, is imagined traveling from China to the Moon. The journey is made in a feathered flying machine called the *Consolidator.* In letter-form the Chinese writes satire of European society and politics, which he compares with lunar conditions.

11. 1709. [MANLEY, DELARIVIERE]. *Secret Memoirs and Manners of several Persons of Quality of Both Sexes from the New Atlantis an Island in the Mediterranean.*

Mrs. Manley uses a device in her Memoirs that suggests the imaginary foreigner. Her travelers come from another world to view England, which is disguised as an imaginary country. The device is not used, as in *The Citizen of the World,* for a point of view from which to criticize, but as an excuse to drag out scandals for the reader's delectation.

12. [1710?] HILLIER, A. *A Brief and Merry History of Great Britain, Containing an account of the religious customs, etc. . . . . of the people, written originally in*

---

[12] Forster, as well as Prior, calls attention to the fact that there is a similarity of plan in Swift's projected book and Goldsmith's *Chinese Letters.* See Forster, *Life and Times of Oliver Goldsmith* I. 252.

Arabick [by Ali Mohammed Hadjii, pseud.]. *Faith-fully rendered into English by A. H.* [A. Hillier], London.

A Brief and Merry History resembles *The Citizen of the World* in its being an account of English manners and customs by an Occidental, who poses in the guise of an Oriental. The author sometimes compares Britain to his native land, praising the latter, and condemning the former in the most vindictive manner.

13. 1710. STEELE, RICHARD. *The Tatler*, No. 56.

In *Tatler*, No. 56, Richard Steele introduces a foreigner of unidentified nationality, who understands the English language imperfectly. This foreigner makes no observations upon England, but 'the questions he asks about the persons of figure' met in public places furnish a reason for Steele's satirical comments on 'sharpers'.

14. 1713. ADDISON, JOSEPH. *The Spectator* No. 512.

Miss Conant suggests, in her *Oriental Tale in England*,[13] that *Chinese Letter*, No. C,[14] which appeared in the *Public Ledger*, January 5, 1761, was possibly suggested to Goldsmith by Addison's *Spectator*, No. 512, Friday, October 17, 1713. She summarizes Goldsmith's essay in the following way:[15] 'Injustice thwarted by quick wit is illustrated in the conclusion of the story of the clever prime minister. Unjustly accused of misgovernment, he asked to be banished to a desolate village.' His queen granted the request, but could find no such village. Hence she realized

---

[13] P. 195, note 1.

[14] The issue of the *Public Ledger* which contains Letter C is missing from the British Museum files; this letter is *The Citizen of the World*, Letter CI.

[15] P. 195.

the universal prosperity of the country under her vizier's rule, and withdrew the unjust accusation.

Addison's fable of injustice thwarted by quick wit has this resemblance to Goldsmith's story: A clever Vizier to the great Sultan Mahmoud pointed out to his sovereign, by repeating a conversation of the birds, whose language he pretended to have learned, the injustice of a reign which allowed the villages of the land to fall into desolation. When the Sultan learned that the owls were settling a wedding portion of five hundred of his ruined villages upon their children, he immediately 'rebuilt the Towns and Villages which had been destroyed, and from that time forth consulted the good of his people.' [16]

15. 1717. *The Conduct of Christians made the sport of Infidels, in a letter from a Turkish Merchant at Amsterdam to the Grand Mufti at Constantinople on occasion of . . . the late scandalous quarrel among the clergy* [by Kora Selym Oglan, pseud.], London, 1717.

The Conduct of Christians is a satirical pseudo-letter.

16. 1714. *The Muscovite.*[17]

The Muscovite is a periodical, the general plan of which resembles *The Citizen of the World.* The first number was printed on May 5, 1714; successive numbers continued weekly. It 'professes to comprise the Reflections of a Muscovite, under the feigned name of Plescon, on subjects which, while travelling through the most civilized countries, had occurred to his observations'.

[16] See *Spectator,* ed. 1713, pp. 206-7.
[17] See *Catalogue of a Collection of Early Newspapers and Essayists * * * presented to the Bodleian Library by the late Rev. Frederick William Hope,* M.A., D.C.L., Oxford: Clarendon Press, 1865, p. 29, No. 108.

17. 1714. *The Spectator*, No. 557.[18]

Addison quotes in *Spectator*, No. 557, a letter alleged to have been written in King Charles II's reign by the ambassador of Bantam, shortly after his arrival in England. The topic under discussion is the insincerity of polite but meaningless expressions among the English. Addison points out the absurdity of effusive begging of 'ten thousand pardons,' of offering to do 'any service that lies in one's power,' of being 'eternally obliged,' and of demanding 'how-do-you-do above a hundred times a day.' He brings ridicule upon such exaggerated politeness by describing the anger of an Englishman who had just promised to be 'eternally obliged' to the Bantamese ambassador when that dignitary, believing the words, demanded so simple a request as the loan of the Englishman's daughter for the short period of two weeks. Of course this incident aims not only to point fun at the insincerity of 'gentile' manners, but also to entertain the reader by the attitude of the Oriental traveler.

It will be remembered that Goldsmith treated the same theme for which the concrete source has been pointed out.[19] Addison's essay does not supply specific material.

18. 1724. DEFOE, DANIEL. *A Tour Through England*.

'Defoe's *Tour Through England*, though not a satire, is connected with the *genre* of pseudo-letters in being written as if by a foreigner.'[20]

19. 1725. GUEULLETTE, THOMAS SIMON. *Chinese Tales*.[21]

Thomas Simon Gueullette was one of the most prolific writers of French pseudo-translations whose works were

---

[18] Dated June 21, 1714.
[19] See above, p. 43.
[20] Conant, *op. cit.*, p. 200.
[21] *Chinese Tales, or the wonderful Adventures of the Mandarin, Fum-Hoam, translated from the French* of T. S. Gueullette. London, 1725.

of sufficient popularity to demand that they be done into English.

The scheme of his *Chinese Tales* is novel and interesting. The tales deal with the successive transmigrations of Fum-Hoam's soul, which enters a different body in each story; for example: a flea's, a monkey's, a dog's, a maid's, a tyrant's, and a bat's. The various stories are held together by an ingenious frame-tale. The work is almost entirely one of narrative appeal.

There are no similarities of detail between this work and *The Citizen of the World,* except in the name of the Mandarin Fum-Hoam, which may have been drawn from this source.[22]

20. 1728. *The Flying-Post: or, the Weekly Medley.* French and English. By a society of Gentlemen. No. 1, Saturday, October 5, 1728.

'Montalaya, a native of Hayatamar, a little city near Medina, settled at Bagdat in the Trade of Selling Pitchers; in the process of time his Poetry, and especially his Philosophy, gain'd him very great Applause.' The first number of *The Flying-Post* contains the imaginary-observer device.

21. 1730. GOMEZ, MME. MADELEINE ANGELIQUE (POISSON) DE. *Persian Anecdotes; or, Secret Memoirs of the Court in Persia. Written originally in French, for the Entertainment of the King, by the celebrated Madame de Gomez, Author of La Belle Assemblée.* Translated by Paul Chamberlain, Gent. London, 1730.

Madame Gomez' *Persian Anecdotes* bears a resemblance to the pseudo-letter *genre* only in its pretense to be an authentic Persian story.

[22] Miss Conant has made the same conjecture.

22. 1731. *The Hyp-Doctor,* No. 10. By Sir Isaac Rat-
cliffe, of Elbow Lane. 'A consult of the Hyps on a
better Hague Letter than t'other, written by *Abdel
Melec,* a *Turkish* Physician, attending the *Turkish
young* Nobleman, so much talk'd of, to his Friend,
Hamet Ben Omar, at *Scutari,* near *Constantinople,*
a spurious Copy of which was published in the Dutch
Gazette; . . . . done from the Original *Arabic,* by
Mr. *John Oldcastle,* Secretary to L—d B—ke, and
Drugger man, that is, Interpreter to Mr. P—t—y.'

The Hyp-Doctor, No. 11, contains a pseudo-Letter supposedly written by a Cherokee Indian to Eustace Budgell.
It has both satirical and descriptive aspects.

23. 1731. *Milk for Babes, Meat for Strong Men, and
Wine for Petitioners, being a Comical, Sarcastic,
Theological Account of a later Election at Bagdad
for Cailiff of that City.* Faithfully Translated from
the Arabick and Collated with the most Authentick
Original Manuscripts by the Great, Learned, and
Most Ingenious Alexander the Coppersmith [W.
Boles?], . . . Second edition, Cork, 1731.

Milk for Babes resembles the device used in *The Citizen
of the World* only in being a satire which, although originally written in English, is asserted to be a translation
from an Oriental tongue; and in giving a pseudo-account
of Oriental conditions.

24. 1736. Locatelli, Francesco, Count. *Lettres Muscovites; or Muscovian Letters. Containing an
account of the form of Government, Customs, and
Manners of that great Empire. Written by an Italian
officer of Distinction* [i. e. Count F. Locatelli.]
Translated from the French . . . by W. Musgrave.
London, 1736.

Locatelli's *Muscovian Letters* use *The Citizen of the World*
device only in part. That is, they are satiric and critical

letters written by a foreigner, about a land which he is visiting. They do not pretend to be translations from the tongue of the foreigner into the tongue of the nation subjected to criticism.

25. 1737. *Letters from a Moore at London to his Friend at Tunis. Containing an Account of his Journey through England; with his Observations on the Laws, Customs, Religion and Manners of the English Nation. Likewise Remarks on the Public Charities. . . . The whole interspersed with Historical Remarks and useful Observations.* The Seventh Edition. London, 1740. [Edited by William Lloyd.]

The general scheme of Lloyd's *Letters from a Moore at London* is the one commonly adopted by the writers of pseudo-letters. A Moor who travels through England writes observations to his friend at Tunis. The remarks made are in essence such as one finds in guide-books. Public buildings in the cities are listed and described; English institutions are didactically commented upon. There is little philosophic or reflective criticism; and there is but scant comment on English conduct; satire is negligible; narrative appeal is barely attempted. Lloyd's work is, for the most part, a book of facts, for the use of foreign travelers in England.

26. 1744. BOYER (JEAN BAPTISTE DE), MARQUIS D' ARGENS. *The Jewish Spy: Being a Philosophical, Historical, and critical correspondence by Letters which lately pass'd between certain JEWS in Turkey, Italy, France, &c. Translated from the Originals into French, By the Marquis D' Argens; and now done into English.* The Second Edition. London, 1744.

D'Argens' *Jewish Spy,* a work in six volumes, is, like his *Chinese Letters,* a contribution to the pseudo-letter *genre.*

In this case a Jew, Aaron Monceca, who was brought up with philosophical training at Constantinople, corresponds from Paris with friends in Turkey, and elsewhere, who reply generously to his epistles. The letters are avowedly written in Hebrew, and D'Argens, in giving a French version to the public, makes pretense that he translates it from that language. Slight narrative interest is attempted

Aside from the general similarity of the device used, there are no points of resemblance between the *Jewish Spy* and Goldsmith's *Chinese Letters*.

27. 1744. *The Meddler*, No. 11. Printed at Dublin. Possibly edited or conducted by William Rufus Chetwood.

The Meddler, No. 11, contains the foreign observer device. Satire of social customs is written by a Persian in Ireland to his friend in Sheraz.

28. 1745. VIEUX-MAISONS, MME. DE, or PECQUET, A. (?). *The Perseis, or secret memoirs for a History of Persia* [a political satire], *translated from the French with a key.* . . . London, 1745.

This work is distantly connected with *The Citizen of the World* device, in being a satire of Persia by an Englishman who resided at Ispahan. The French original asserts that it is a translation from an English work.

29. 1749. GRAFFIGNY, F. HUGUET DE. *Letters written by a Peruvian Princess, translated from the French* [of F. Huguet de Graffigny]. London, 1748.

Mme. de Graffigny's *Letters written by a Peruvian Princess* are built upon this general scheme: A Peruvian princess, captured by the Spaniards, comes by force of circumstances to France, where, released from captivity, she reflects on the virtues of her own country and country-men, and on the evils of France and Frenchmen. These reflections she writes to Aza, her brother. She also addresses other persons; but no replies are received. The correspondence is supposedly translated into French by Madame de Graffigny.

30. 1749 or 1750. DODD, DR. WILLIAM. *The African Prince now in England, to Zara at his Father's Court and Zara's Answer.*[23]

Dr. Dodd's *African Prince now in England* bears the following resemblances to *The Citizen of the World:* it consists of pseudo-letters, which pretend to be translations from an Oriental tongue by the editor of the epistles; the letter from the African prince is satirically critical of England, the nation visited.

31. 1755. *The Friend*, No. 8.

Contains the foreign-observer device.

32. 1755. SHEBBEARE, JOHN. *Letters on the English Nation: By Batista Angeloni, a Jesuit, Who resided many years in London. Translated from the Original Italian, by the Author of the Marriage Act, a Novel.* London, 1755

The Letters on the English Nation by John Shebbeare are pseudo-epistles in descriptive, critical, and sometimes satirical vein. They often refer to the Chinese fad which was sweeping over England at the time of their composition; and they may have been of considerable inspiration to Goldsmith in showing the universality of interest which would attach to a work that dealt with China.

[23] Watt dates this work 1750. The *Dictionary of National Biography* gives 1749.

33. 1760. *The Visitor*, No. 17.[24]

Contains the foreign-observer device.

34. 1760-1. *The Algerine Spy.*

Embraces twenty-four letters, descriptive and narrative, written from Philadelphia by an Algerine, to
correspondents at Algiers.

NOTES

These notes are designed to indicate the character and
extent of Goldsmith's use of Le Comte and Du Halde as
source-books for his Oriental allusions.[25]

[Louis Le Comte was one of the six Jesuit missionaries sent to China in 1685 by the King of France.
After his return to France he published the *Nouveaux
Mémoires aur l' Etat Présent de la Chine*, 1696. This
work was frequently reprinted in France, and was
translated in England.

Père Du Halde, another Jesuit missionary, who
passed thirty-two years of his life in the Orient, published the *Histoire Générale de la Chine*, 1735. It is a
geographical, historical, and social account of China
written by himself, containing contributions from
twenty-seven other missionaries.

From these two works Goldsmith obtained nearly
all his knowledge of China.][26]

[24] Appeared in the *Public Ledger*, Vol. 1, No. 138, June 20, 1760.
[25] Because of the inaccessibility of the *Public Ledger*, the references are given to Gibbs' edition of *The Citizen of the World*. The
first figure refers to the page, and the second to the line. Important
differences between the *Public Ledger* text and *The Citizen of the
World* have been collated.

[26] It is established beyond a doubt, by comparison of texts and
page-references, that Goldsmith used the English translations of these
works. In one case the French version of Le Comte is referred to
by Goldsmith, but in general he used the translation. In all cases,
I have compared *The Citizen of the World* with both the English
translation and the French original.

9. 17. How comes it, said they, that the Europeans. . . reason just as we do.

How can it possibly be, said they, *that a People so far remote from us, should have any Wit or Capacity. They have never perused our Books; they were never modelled by our Laws, and yet they speak, discourse, and argue aright as we do.*—Le Comte, p. 121.

13. 7. Honan.

This province is situated near the middle of China. See Du Halde 1. 214.

13. 8. mandarine.

A full account of the various orders of mandarins, of their rank and duties, is given by Du Halde 2. 32 ff.

15. 34. Nankin.

This city was one of the wealthiest and most prosperous in China. See Du Halde 1. 133.

19. 37. the small-footed perfections of an Eastern beauty.

'But that which distinguishes them from all the Women in the World . . . is the littleness of their Feet, and here lyes the most essential point of their Beauty. . . . So soon as ever Girls are born, the Nurses take great care to tye their Feet extream hard that they may not grow.'—Le Comte, p. 125. 'Among the Charms of the Sex the smallness of their Feet is not the least.'—Du Halde 2. 139.

19. 39. the beauties of my native city. . . .How broad their faces; how very short their noses. See Du Halde 2. 138.

29. 9.   Tien, the Universal Soul.

'The chief Object of their [the ancient Chinese] worship is the Supreme Being. . . or *Tien,* which, according to the *Chinese,* signifies the same thing.'—Du Halde 3. 16.

31. 18-9.   Our greatest glory is, not in never falling, but in rising every time we fall.

'In the State wherein we are, Perseverance in Well-doing consists not so much in not falling, as in rising again as often as we fall.'—Le Comte, p. 208.

35. 13-20.   Sure thou has been nurtured by the bill of the Shin Shin, or . . . Gin Hiung . . . Choug Fou. . . Boh that lives in the midst of the waters.

See Du Halde, 1. 20. and comments on this subject, p. 155.

39. 25-6.   The religion of the Daures is more absurd than even that of the sectaries of Fohi.   Also:

54. 25.   Fohi spreads his gross superstitions here also.

'Fo hi . . is acknowledged to be Founder of the *Chinese* Monarchy.'—Du Halde, 3. 21. 'For the Fear of *Chang ti* they [the followers of Fohi] were desirous of substituting the Fear of Spirits, and so had recourse to Magick and Enchantments; they pretended to disturb Houses with malignant Spirits, and terrified the People with their Delusions: The People assembled in the Temple on solemn Days that the Emperor sacrificed, made it resound with their Clamours, tumultously requiring that Sacrifices should likewise be offered to these Spirits."—Du Halde, 3. 23.   See also *The Citizen of the World,* pp. 61, 159.   For a further account of the abominations and superstitions of the sect of Fohi, see Du Halde, 3. 271-2; Le Comte, p. 39.

44. 11. The Chinese . . . hate to die, and they confess their terrors . . . funeral.

'The uncommon Love of Life is another Foible of the *Chinese* Nation; there is scarce any People that are so fond of Living as they . . . acquaint them with it.'—Du Halde 2. 134-5.

65. 69. (Letter XVIII).

Goldsmith's entire letter is a paraphrase of a Chinese *novel*, quoted from Du Halde 3. 134-155. For discussion of Goldsmith's plagiarism, see above, pp. 125-9.

67. 3. a lady dressed in the deepest mourning (being clothed all over in white).

353. 3. The mourning colour of Europe is black; that of China, white.

'The Mourning Habit [of the Chinese] hath also something odd in it. The Bonnet, Vests, Sourtout, Stockings and Boots, are made of white Linnen, and from the Prince to the most inferiour Handicrafts-man, none dare wear any of another colour.' Le Comte, p. 144. 'The Colour of their Mourning is white.'—Du Halde 2. 213.

76. 5. the Chinese who measures his wisdom by the length of his nails.

'Their Doctors, and other Learned Men, let their Nails grow excessively, insomuch that in some they are little shorter than their Fingers; it obtains amongst them not only for an Ornament, but a Distinction, by which it may be known, that by their Condition they are separated from Mechanick Arts, and are wholly addicted to Sciences.'— Le Comte, p. 135; see Du Halde 2. 138.

82. 20-21.   *True magnanimity consists . . . but in RISING*
          every time we fall.

See above note, 31. 18-9.

87. 25.   feast of the Lanterns.

The Feast of the Lanterns is one of the two great festivals of China.   See Le Comte, pp. 161-9; Du Halde 2.165 ff.

93. 22.   ginseng.

Gin seng is an herb of great commercial value.   For an account of its appearance and uses, see Le Comte, pp. 225-6; Du Halde 2. 261; 4. 1 ff.

111. 25-6.   By my last advices from Moscow, I find the caravan has not yet departed for China.

Goldsmith indicates that Altangi's letters to Fum Hoam would be received in batches, because of the infrequent passing of the caravans between Moscow and Pekin.   According to Father Thomas, these left yearly, and took a period of four months in transit.   See Le Comte, p. 11.

125 24-25.   bear's claws . . . . bird's nests.

An account of Chinese food delicacies is given by Du Halde.   He mentions bird's nests as one of their most delicious articles of food.—Du Halde 2. 201.   'Bears are also very common; the Feet of these . . . are delicious Food for the *Chinese.*'—Du Halde 1. 229.   See also *The Citizen of the World,* p. 357.

149. 25.   From Yaoua to Yaya.

The ceremonies of a Chinese call, as shown by Goldsmith, are very elaborate.   A full account of the proper conduct for visits among the Chinese is given by Le Comte, pp. 272-3, and by Du Halde 2. 184 ff.

149. 33. seventeen books of ceremonies.

The whole fabric of Chinese life is built upon the elaborate ceremonies which all classes of people follow out with the greatest punctiliousness. See Du Halde 2. 169-223.

151. 19. eight letters of good fortune.

These are called by the Chinese the *pa-kua;* they are cut out of precious stones or metals, and worn about the neck.

151. 26. *fong whang.*

'The *Fong hoang* is a very scarce Bird, or rather a Fiction, much as our *Phœnix;* according to the *Chinese* Description, he resembles an Eagle, but excells him in the great Variety of his colours.'—Du Halde 1. 278. A description of a copper and silver-gilt fong whang, used as a head-dress, follows.

158. 1. an ancient, extended empire.

For an account of the antiquity of China, see Du Halde 2. 1-3.

158.3-15. The duty of children to their parents . . . the Emperor is the protector, father, and friend.

The whole system of Chinese government is based on the principle of obedience, on obedience of the son to the father, the father to the state, the mandarins, and the emperor. See Le Comte, p 277. Du Halde (2. 32 ff.) discusses the subject at greater length. See p. 101.

158. 26. Emperor Tisiang.

The fifth emperor of the dynasty of Hia. The story which Goldsmith tells of this emperor is not given by Du Halde; it occurs, however, in Le Comte. See Du Halde 1. 290; Le Comte, pp. 267-9. For an account of Goldsmith's use of the passage, and for Le Comte's text, see pp. 89-90.

159. 1.   Emperor Ginsong.

The Emperor Gin tsong was the fourth emperor of the dynasty of Yuen. The story which Goldsmith tells concerning him is taken from Du Halde 1. 447. For a discussion of this matter, see p. 100.

159. 10.   Haitong, the last emperor of the House of Ming.

According to Du Halde, Hoai tsong was the sixteenth and last emperor of the dynasty of Ming. The story related of him by Goldsmith is given by both Le Comte and Du Halde, but in it the author more closely follows the latter. For further discussion, see p. 101. The original texts are to be had in Le Comte, pp. 17-8; in Du Halde 1. 478 ff. A shorter account of the same is given by Du Halde 2. 4-5.

159. 23-34.   An empire which has . . . on the comparison.

This passage should be compared with Du Halde 2. 6. A somewhat different account is given by Le Comte, pp. 19-20. Consult also p. 100.

159.   The disciples of Lao-Kium, the idolatrous sectaries of Fohi, and the philosophical children of Confucius.

'THERE are three principal Sects in the Empire of *China;* the Sect of the Learned, who follow the Doctrine of the ancient Books, and look upon *Confucius* as their Master; that of the Disciples of *Lao kien,* which is nothing but a Web of Extravagance and Impiety; and that of Idolators, who worship a Divinity called *Fo,* whose Opinions were translated from the *Indies* into *China* about thirty-two Years after the Crucifixion of our Saviour.'—From 'Religion of the Chinese,' Du Halde 3. 14.

211. 5-6. You have left it to geographers . . . disposition of the people.

This is only one of many instances in which Goldsmith emphasizes the differences between his *Chinese Letters* and the geographical records of Le Comte and Du Halde.

211. 26-30. We are not to be astonished, says Confucius, . . . while wisdom only points out the way.

'One ought not to wonder that the wise Man walks slower in the Way to Vertue, that the ill Man does in that of Vice, Passion hurries, and Wisdom guides.'—Le Comte, p. 207. See above p. 87. From a note in *The Public Ledger* of July 8, 1760, it is apparent that in this case Goldsmith used the original French version of Le Comte; but in other cases, perhaps in the majority of cases, he used the English translation; for he refers to passages which are included only in that version. Goldsmith's note reads: 'Tho' this fine maxim be not found in the Latin edition of the morals of Confucius, yet we find it ascribed to him by Le Comte, 'Etat present de la Chine,' Vol. 1., p. 348.' *Public Ledger,* July 8, 1760.

239. 31. Yau.

Yao was the eighth emperor of China. 'He is esteemed the first Legislator in the Nation, and the Pattern of Sovereigns.' He is credited with having introduced the intercalation of the lunar year. See Du Halde 1. 283.

239. 32. Confucius and Pythagoras seem born nearly together.

Confucius was born in the forty-seventh year of the thirtieth cycle, in the reign of Ling vang, the twenty-third emperor of China. [The thirtieth cycle began B. C. 597.] See Du Halde 1. 329; Le Comte, pp. 194 ff.

240. 1. Emperor Yonglo.

Tching sou or Yong lo, the third emperor of the twenty-first dynasty, named Ming, reigned with great wisdom for twenty-three years. According to Du Halde, he was a prince of great spirit and uncommon sagacity. See Du Halde 1. 455.

248. 10. Mencius.

Meng tsee, or Mencius, was the most illustrious disciple of Confucius, and as a philosopher was second only to his master. He was born B. C. 435, during the reign of Lie vang, the thirty-first emperor of China. See Du Halde 1. 335.

254. 1. The Chinese boast their skill in pulses.

For an account of the Chinese knowledge of medicine, of the physicians in China, and of the numerous quack doctors, see Le Comte, pp. 215 ff., but especially below, 257. 17.

257. 17. the doctrines of old Wang-shu-ho.

A Chinese medical book, entitled *The Secret of the Pulse*, written by Ouang chou ho, who lived under the dynasty of Tsin (several hundred years before the Christian era) is reprinted in translation by Du Halde 3. 365 ff. See above, pp. 137-8.

272. 5-7. The English laws punish vice; the Chinese laws do more,—they reward virtue.

'Of the Chinese Form of Government, the different Tribunals,' Du Halde 2. 36-72. Cf. *The Vicar of Wakefield*, Chapter 26, chapter heading: 'A reformation in the gaol. To make laws complete they should reward as well as punish.'

277. 21.   Chinvang the Chaste.

Tching ting vang was the twenty-seventh emperor of the dynasty called Tcheou. 'After the Death of the Empress he liv'd in Celibacy, an Example of Continency which was no less admired, than the Rarity of it; from whence he was surnamed the *Chaste*.'—Du Halde 1. 333.

280. 27.   Lama.

The Tartars worshiped this animal as a divinity.   See Du Halde 2. 8.

289. 20-1.   those at Pekin have a board to assure the buyer that they have no intentions to cheat him.

See Du Halde 1. 108; Le Comte, p. 57.   For discussion, see above, p. 103.

295. 8.   scour up her copper tail.

Gibbs (*Works* 3. 395, note 1) says that this is perhaps an allusion to an ornament corresponding with that called the foong-hoâng..   See above, note to 151. 26.

310. 8.   a modern philosopher of China.

The remarks which Goldsmith quotes as those of 'a modern philosopher of China' are taken from Du Halde's 'Translation of a Chinese Author, Containing Precepts of Morality,' which is included in the *General History* 3. 121-356.   Du Halde does not give the name of the author whose tract he translates, but refers to him as a 'modern philoso·pher.'   Goldsmith half acknowledges in this instance that his quotation is taken from Du Halde, for a note which appears in the *Public Ledger,* October 15, 1760, reads: 'A translation of this passage may also be seen in Du Halde, Vol II. p. 47 and 58.   This extract will at least serve to shew that fondness for humour which appears in the writings of the Chinese.' The remarks from the 'modern philosopher' are not, however, to be found only on the pages to which Goldsmith refers; his quotation is something less than a very loose paraphrase which is huddled together from several pages of the 'Translation of a Chinese Author.' Cf. especially Du Halde 3. 113, 141, 353, 355; 4. 510. For discussion of this matter, see above, p. 140 ff.

311. 33.   except romances.

'The sentiments here are very like Goldsmith's own on the same subject, in his letter to his brother, the Rev. Henry Goldsmith (1759), thus (see our vol. 1. p. 449): "Above all things let him [Henry's son] never touch a romance or novel; these paint beauty in colours more charming than nature, and describe happiness that man never tastes. How delusive, how destructive, are those pictures of consummate bliss! They teach the youthful mind to sigh after beauty and happiness which never existed; to despise the little good which fortune has mixed in our cup, by expecting more than she ever gave." Yet the above, it will be seen, purports to be a passage from a "modern philosopher of China," which is also translated in Du Halde.' (*Works,* ed. Gibbs, 3. 311, note 1.)

Gibbs is quite right; the sentiments expressed in this passage were undoubtedly Goldsmith's, but in writing the passage he also undoubtedly made a loose paraphrase of the sentiments which Du Halde quotes from 'the modern philosopher.' See Du Halde 4. 510.

312. 3-19.   The most indecent strokes. . . the most dangerous attacks.

Cf.   'There are a sort of Women. . . sometimes they sing Verses, sometimes relate a Story. . . this Custom observed.' Du Halde 3. 356, but especially 3. 113.

312.21. vice punished and virtue rewarded.

'This looks almost as if "the modern philosopher of China" had had the English Samuel Richardson in his "mind's eye." Knight's edition of "The Citizen of the World" stands alone in printing the quotation from the "modern philosopher of China" as ending three paragraphs back—with "unabating assiduity"—which arrangement gives the remarks about "romances" and "virtue rewarded" to Goldsmith, to whom they really seem to belong; yet all the early editions, including the *Ledger* edition, and all later editions, save Knight's, have the quotation marked as if coming down to the end of the letter' (*Works,* ed. Gibbs, 3. 312, note 1). Gibbs is wrong in supporting Knight; the other editions are correct in their quotation. If Gibbs had consulted Du Halde, he would have found the passages which Goldsmith acknowledges concerning romances (see above, notes on 310. 8; 311. 33; 312. 3-19.) The passage concerning 'virtue rewarded' may have been suggested by Du Halde's remarks about Chinese 'novels'; although it does not occur in the quotation from the 'modern philosopher.' See Du Halde 3. 113. It is certainly not improbable that, in writing this passage, Goldsmith had Richardson in mind.

319. 33. the seventeen books of Chinese ceremonies.

The elaborate ceremonies of the Chinese were written in many books. In his *General History* (2. 169-223), Du Halde gives a long account of the various ceremonies. From this section Goldsmith frequently drew in composing the *Chinese Letters*. See above, note on 149. 25.

334. 17-35. assures us, that China was peopled by a colony from Egypt . . . therefore the Chinese are a colony from Egypt.

This story about the foundation of the Chinese is not found in Le Comte or Du Halde; but the theory expounded

in the next paragraph (see below, note on 334. 37-8) is
found in the latter author's *General History*.   A burlesque
of pedantry similar to Goldsmith's occurs in Voltaire's
article 'Chine' in the *Dictionnaire Philosophique*.   The
pertinent portion of that article reads (*Dict. Phil.*, ed.
Garnier Frères, p. 141): 'Dans une province d'Occident,
nommée autrefois *la Celtique,* on a poussé le gût de la singu-
larité & du paradoxe jusqu' à dire que les Chinois n' étaient
qu' une colonie d' Egypte, ou bien, si l' on veut, de Phénicie.
On a cru prouver, comme on prouve tant d'autre choses,
qu'un Roi d' Egypte appelé *Ménès* par les grecs, était le roi
de la Chine *Yu,* & qu' *Atoes* etait *Ki,* en changeant seule-
ment quelques lettres.'

334. 31.   Emperor Ki.

The seventeenth and last emperor of the first dynasty.
See Du Halde 1. 296; Le Comte, p. 165.

334. 34.   Emperor Yu.

The first emperor of the first dynasty, B. C. 2217.   See
Du Halde 1. 286.

334. 37-8.   he will have the Chinese to be a colony planted
        by Noah.

'IT is a common Opinion, and almost universally received
among those who have searched after the Original of an
Empire so ancient as *China,* that the SONS of *Noah* were
scattered abroad in the Eastern Part of *Asia;* that some of
the Descendants of this Patriarch penetrated into *China*
about two hundred Years after the Deluge, and laid the
Foundation of this vast Monarchy.'—Du Halde 3. 15.

341. 19-23.   In China, if two porters should meet in a nar-
        row street . . . on their knees.

'THE *Chinese* are . . . mild, tractable, and humane; there is a great deal of Affability in their Air and Manner, and nothing harsh, rough, or passionate. . . . I was one Day. . . in a long Lane, where there happened in a short time a great Stop of Carriages; I expected they would have fallen into a Passion, used opprobrious Language, and perhaps have come to Blows, as is very common in *Europe;* but I was much surpriz'd to see that they saluted each other, spoke mildly, as if they had been old Acquaintance, and lent their Mutual Assistance to pass each other.'—Du Halde 2. 128.

352. 8-12. I am mounted upon a wretched ass . . . thank Heaven for my own.

This anecdote is taken from Du Halde (4. 64). See above, p. 106.

352. 13-32. Shingfu, when under misfortunes . . . not a bit of my tongue.

The anecdote told in this paragraph is taken from Du Halde, who relates it as part of a dialogue between the philosopher Lao tse and his disciples. It is contained in a long Chinese writing quoted in translation by Du Halde. This writing is entitled, *A Dialogue Wherein Tchin, a modern Chinese Philosopher, declares his Opinion concerning the Origin and State of the World.* In it Tchin vou discusses religion and other matters with a crowd of young men, adherents of the sect of Fo. The text which Goldsmith paraphrased from Du Halde is quoted above on p. 107, but see also Du Halde 3. 257, 264. It should be noticed that the name Shinfu, which Goldsmith uses, is merely an orthographic change from the original Tchin vou, as it appears in the *Dialogue.*

353. 2-3. The mourning colour of Europe is black; that of China, white.

See above, note on 67. 3.

353. 9 to 354. 4. On the contrary, with us in China . . . at least we are taught to regret them for our own.

This account of a Chinese funeral frequently follows the phraseology of Du Halde's description, which reads, in part, as follows (2. 215-8):

'On each side [of a table before the coffin of the deceased] are placed, in several Ranks, a great Number of Figures of Officers, Eunuchs, Soldiers, Lions, saddled Horses, Camels, Tortoises, and other animals in different Attitudes, with Signs of Grief and Veneration in their Aspects. . . .

'The Coffin is exposed in the principal Room, adorned with white Stuff . . . surrounded with Flowers, Perfumes, and lighted Wax-candles.

'Those who come to make their Compliments of Condolence salute the Deceased after the manner of their Country, that is, they prostrate themselves, and beat their Foreheads several times against the Ground before the Table, on which they afterwards place the Wax-Candles and Perfumes. . . . Those who were particular Friends accompany these Ceremonies with Tears and Groans, which may be heard at a great distance. . . .

'When the Ceremony is ended they rise up, and a distant Relation of the Deceased . . . conducts them into another Apartment. . . .

'The eldest Son . . . together with the Grandchildren, follow on Foot covered with a hempen Sack. . . .

'Nothing can be more surprising than the Tears which the *Chinese* shed, and the Cries that they make at these Funerals; but as every thing seems to be done to an *European* in exact Order, and according to Rule, the Affectation wherewith they seem to express their Sorrow is not capable of exciting in him the same Sentiments of Grief that he is Spectator of.'

353. 25.   For two long months did this mourning continue.

The *Public Ledger* (October 29, 1760) has 'two years,' which Gibbs (*Works* 3. 353, note 2) says is perhaps a misprint. According to Du Halde (2. 216), however, corpses were sometimes kept three or four years above ground.

357-28.   assafœtida.

Assafœtida, a promoter of digestion somewhat resembling garlic, was much used in cooking Chinese dishes.   See Le Comte and Du Halde, *passim*.

363. 29-31.   instead of one soul, Fohi, the idol of China, gives every woman three.

Goldsmith, in a note to the *Public Ledger,* December 29, 1760, quotes Du Halde as the authority for this statement.   He says: 'Vid. Du Halde passim.'   Du Halde, however, nowhere makes the statement that Fohi gives a woman three souls; but he does say (3. 271) that according to the doctrines of the sect of Fo, the 'Trunk of Substance' of man is one, but it has 'three images.'   The theory is applied to mankind, not to woman alone.   The adherents of the sect of Fo also believe that at the resurrection the women shall become men.—Du Halde, 3. 373.

364. 16-28.   Another ceremony, said I . . . *her three days of freedom* . . . one inundation of arrack punch.

The above paragraph Goldsmith paraphrases from Du Halde's translation of an unnamed Chinese author.   See Du Halde, 3. 364.   For comment, and for the text of the Chinese author whom Goldsmith copied, see pp. 108-9.

371. 16 ff. Shang, our maiden aunt, played with a sharper
      . . . became his own.

The passion for gambling among the Chinese is described
by Le Comte, who says that Chinese often stake their entire
fortunes, homes, children, and even their wives, on the
throw of a single card. See Le Comte, p. 292.

376. 21 ff. When Father Matthew. . . Controller.

The inaccuracies of Chinese astronomers are described at
length by Le Comte, pp. 63-5. There was much friction
between the Jesuit missionaries and the Chinese astronomers,
because the latter disliked to be instructed by Europeans.
The emperors, however, frequently encouraged the Jesuits,
especially Father Verbiest, who taught the Chinese much.
For an account of the Chinese skill in astronomy, and of the
relations of the astronomers with the missionaries, see Du
Halde 3. 78-110.

389. 4-21. There is, probably, no country so barbarous
      . . . the sculpture of a cherry stone.

Compare with this Le Comte's account of the missionaries
who were traveling in China, seized by the Chinese, and
made to wait their judgment until the return of the Emperor
to Pekin. See Le Comte, p. 22.

390. 3. the missioner.

Goldsmith here refers to the Jesuit missionaries. Among
the most famous of these were Père Le Comte, Père Du
Halde, Père Matthew Ricci, and Père Verbiest. See Du
Halde 1, preface.

396. 5. our fish.

Gold fish and silver fish are here referred to. See Le
Comte, p. 113; Du Halde 1. 27.

402. 24.   Feast of the Lanterns.

See above, note on 87. 25.

435. 4.   Deputy Mandarine of Macca.

For the various orders of mandarins, see Du Halde 2.
32 ff.   Maccan is the port of the Province of Quang tcheou.

446. 18-9.   They must often change . . . who would be constant in happiness or wisdom.

'A Man ought to change often, if he would be constant in
Wisdom.'—Le Comte, p. 203.

BIBLIOGRAPHY

This bibliography is of the works mentioned in the text. It refers to the edition used by the author. First and early editions are mentioned in notes to the text, and are not listed here unless used by the author.

ADDISON, JOSEPH. *The Spectator*. 9 vols. London, 1713.
———. *Algerine Spy*. London, 1760-1.
ARABIAN NIGHTS ENTERTAINMENTS. London, 1778.
BELLONI. *Il Seicento* (in *Storia Litteraria d'Italia*). Milano, 1898-9.
BOCCALINI, TRAJANO. *I Ragguagli di Parnaso*. London, 1674.
BOYER, JEAN BAPTISTE DE., Marquis D'Argens. *Chinese Letters*. London, 1739.
———. *The Jewish Spy*. London, 1744.
BOYLE, ROBERT. *Occasional Reflections* (in Boyle, *Works*, ed. 1772, Vol. 5.) London, 1772.
BRITISH MAGAZINE. London, 1760-1764.
BROTANEK. *Trajano Boccalini's Einfluss auf die Englische Literatur* (in *Archiv für das Studium der Neueren Sprachen und Litteraturen*, Vol. III, 1903.)
BROWN, THOMAS. *Amusements Serious and Comical*. London, 1707-8.
BYROM, JOHN. *Tom the Porter*, ed. Ward. London, 1894.
CAMPBELL. *The Seven Sages of Rome*. Boston, 1907.
CAPORALI. *Gli Avvisi di Parnaso*. Ferrara, 1590.
———. *Il Viaggio di Parnaso*. Ferrara, 1590.
CAXTON, WILLIAM. *The Game of Chesse*, ed. Smith. London, 1860.
CHAMBERS, WILLIAM. *Designs of Chinese Buildings*. London, 1757.
———. *Dissertation on Oriental Gardening*. London, 1772.
CLEVELAND, JOHN. *Satire on the Scots* (in Cleveland, *Works*, ed. 1699. London).
COLLINS, JAMES. *Oriental Eclogues*. London, 1757.
———. *The Persian Eclogues*. London, 1742.
CONANT, MARTHA. *The Oriental Tale in England in the Eighteenth Century*. New York, 1908.
THE CONDUCT OF CHRISTIANS. London, 1717.
CONFUCIUS. See Couplet.
COUPLET. *Confucius Sinarum Philosophus*. Paris, 1687.
CRITICAL REVIEW. London, 1759.

D'ARGENS. See Boyer.

DEFOE, DANIEL. *The Consolidator.* London, 1705.

———. *Tour Through the Island of Great Britain.* 4 vols. Dublin, 1779.

DICTIONARY OF NATIONAL BIOGRAPHY. 63 vols. London, 1885-1901.

DODD, WILLIAM. *The African Prince.* London, 1749 or 1750.

DRAKE, NATHAN. *The Gleaner.* 4 vols. London, 1811.

DU FRESNY, CHARLES. *Amusements Sérieux et Comiques.* Amsterdam, 1719.

———. *Siamese Letters.* See *Amusements Sérieux et Comiques.*

DU HALDE. *The General History of China.* London, 1736.

———. *Histoire Générale de la Chine,* ed. Scheurleer. La Haye, 1736.

FLAMINI, FRANCESCO. *Studi di Storia Litteraria Italiana e Straniera.* Leghorn, 1895.

FLYING POST, THE. London, 1728.

FORSTER, JOHN. *Life and Times of Oliver Goldsmith.* 2 vols. London, 1855.

FRIEND, THE. London, 1755.

GENTLEMAN'S MAGAZINE, THE. London, 1757-65.

GILDON, CHARLES. *The Post-Boy Robb'd of his Mail.* London, 1706.

GOLDSMITH, OLIVER. *The Bee* (in Goldsmith, *Works,* ed. Gibbs. Vol. 2. London, 1884).

———. *An Enquiry into the Present State of Polite Learning in Europe.* London, 1774.

———. *Chinese Letters* (in *The Public Ledger.* London, 1760-1).

———. *The Citizen of the World.* First ed., London, 1762; Second ed., London, 1769; Third ed.. London, 1774; another ed., Albany, 1794; ed. Percy, London, 1801; ed. Prior, London, 1837; ed. Cunningham, London, 1855; ed. Gibbs, 1884-6; ed. Dobson, London, 1891.

———. *Le Citoyen du Monde,* ed. Poire. Paris, 1764.

———. *Letters* (in Goldsmith, *Works,* ed. Gibbs. London, 1884).

———. *Memoirs of M. de Voltaire* (in Goldsmith, *Works,* ed. Gibbs. London, 1884).

———. *She Stoops to Conquer* (in Goldsmith, *Works,* ed. Gibbs. London, 1884).

———. *Miscellaneous Works,* ed. Percy. London, 1801.

———. *Works,* ed. Prior. London, 1837.

———. *Works,* ed. Cunningham. London, 1855.

———. *Works,* ed. Gibbs. London, 1884-6.

GOMEZ, MME. M. DE. *Persian Anecdotes.* London, 1730.

GRAFFIGNY, MME. DE. *Lettres d'une Péruvienne.* Amsterdam, 1748.
———. *Letters Written by a Peruvian Princess.* London. 1748.
GREENOUGH, C. N. *Review of Miss Conant's Oriental Tale in England. Journal of English and Germanic Philology,* Vol. 8. Champaign, Illinois, 1909.
GUEULLETTE, SIMON. *Chinese Tales.* London, 1725.
———. *Mogul Tales.* London, 1736.
———. *Peruvian Tales.* London, 1764.
———. *Tartarian Tales.* London, 1759.
HALLAM, HENRY. *Introduction to the Literature of Europe.* 3 vols. London, 1854.
HAWKESWORTH. *The Adventurer,* 1752-4.
———. *Almoran and Hamet; an Oriental Tale.* London, 1761.
HERBERT OF CHERBURY, *Autobiography,* ed. Walpole, Strawberry Hill, 1764.
HILLIER, A. *A Brief and Merry History.* London, (1710?).
HOPE, F. W. *Catalogue of a Collection of Early Newspapers.* Oxford, 1865.
HYDE, EDWARD. *Letter to David Mallet* (reprinted in Goldsmith, *Works,* ed. Gibbs. London, 1884).
HYP-DOCTOR, THE. London, 1731.
JOHNSON, SAMUEL. *The Idler.* London, 1767.
———. *The Prince of Abissinia.* London, 1759.
———. *The Rambler.* London, 1779.
———. *Rasselas.* London, 1759. See *The Prince of Abissinia.*
JONES, SIR WM. *Dissertation sur la Littérature Orientale.* London, 1771.
———. *A Grammar of the Persian Language.* London, 1801.
———. *Poeseos Asiaticæ Commentariorum Libri Sex.* London, 1774.
———. *Traité sur la Poésie Orientale.* London, 1770.
JOURNAL OF ENGLISH AND GERMANIC PHILOLOGY. Champaign, Illinois.
KAEMPFER, ENGELBERTUS. *The History of Japan.* London, 1728.
KING, WILLIAM. *A Journey to London.* Reprinted in *A Miscellany of the Wits,* ed. Colville. London, 1920.
LADIES MAGAZINE, THE. London, 1761.
LE COMTE. *Memoirs and Observations.* London, 1698.
———. *Nouveaux Mémoires sur l'Etat Présent de la Chine.* Paris, 1697.
L'ESPION A FRANKFORT. Paris, 1741.

L'ESPION CHINOIS EN EUROPE. Paris, 1745.

LETTERS FROM AN ARMENIAN IN IRELAND. London, 1756.

LETTERS FROM A MOORE AT LONDON, ed. Lloyd. London, 1740.

LOCATELLI. *Lettres Muscovites.* London, 1736.

LYTTELTON, GEORGE. *Letters from a Persian in England.* London, 1744.

MANLEY. *The Secret Memoirs . . . . from The New Atlantis.* 2 vols. 2d ed. London, 1709.

MARANA. *L'Espion Turc.* Paris, 1684.

————. *Letters Writ by a Turkish Spy.* London, 1687-93.

MEDDLER, THE. London, 1744.

MILK FOR BABES. London, 1731.

MEMORIALS OF MRS. GILBERT. London, 1874.

MONTESQUIEU. *Letters Persanes* (in *Œuvres de Montesquieu.* Paris, 1764).

————. *Persian Letters.* London, 1730.

MONTHLY REVIEW, THE. London, 1760-4.

MONBRON, FOUGERET DE. *Le Cosmopolite.* Paris, 1750.

MURPHY. *The Orphan of China.* London, 1759.

MUSCOVITE, THE. London, 1714.

MISCELLANEOUS PIECES RELATING TO THE CHINESE, ed. Percy. 2 vols. London, 1762.

PUBLIC LEDGER, THE. London, 1760-61.

PLUTARCH.

PRIOR, JAMES. *Life of Goldsmith.* 2 vols. London, 1837.

PUCKLE. *England's Path to Wealth and Honour.* London, 1700.

ROYAL MAGAZINE, THE. London, 1760-64.

SHEBBEARE, JOHN. *Letters on the English Nation.* London, 1755.

SMOLLETT, TOBIAS. *Adventures of Sir Launcelot Greaves.* In the *British Magazine.* London. 1760-1.

STERNE, LAURENCE. *The Life and Opinions of Tristram Shandy, Gentleman.* 9 vols. in 3. London, 1760-7.

SWIFT, JONATHAN. *Journal to Stella,* ed. Ryland. London, 1897.

TALE OF A TUB, A. London, 1704.

TOLDO. *Dell' Espion di Giovanni Paolo Marana.* (In *Giornale Storico,* 1887.)

VIEUX MAISONS. *The Perseis.* London, 1745.

VISITOR, THE. London, 1760.

VOLTAIRE. [F. M. Arouet de.] *Mélanges.* (In *Œuvres Complètes de Voltaires,* ed. Garnier Frères. Paris, 1877-85.)

————. *Œuvres Complètes de Voltaire.* ed. Garnier Frères. Toms. 52. Paris, 1877-85. For all references to Voltaire, see this edition.

WALPOLE, HORACE. *The Castle of Otranto, A Gothic Story.* Parma, 1791.
——. *Letters.* ed. Mrs. Paget Toynbee. 2 vols. Oxford, 1915.
——. *A Letter from Xo-Ho.* London, 1757.
WARD. *The London Spy.* London, 1703.
WILKINSON, J. *Hau Kiou Chooan,* a Translation from the Chinese. [Ed. by T. Percy.] London, 1761.
ZOROASTER. *Zend-Avesta,* tr. Anquetil du Perron. 3 tom. Paris, 1771.